Grill made by a Group of Students working under the Instruction
of the Author of this Book

DECORATIVE WROUGHT IRONWORK
Projects for Beginners

THOMAS F. GOOGERTY

DOVER PUBLICATIONS, INC.
Mineola, New York

Bibliographical Note

This Dover edition, first published in 2005, is an unabridged republication of the work originally published by The Manual Arts Press, Peoria, Illinois, in 1937 under the title *Decorative Wrought Iron Work / Working Drawings and Working Notes on the Making of Simple, / Useful Articles from Wrought Iron, Brass and Copper.*

Library of Congress Cataloging-in-Publication Data

Googerty, Thomas F. (Thomas Francis), b. 1865.
  [Decorative wrought iron work.]
  Decorative wrought ironwork projects for beginners / Thomas F. Googerty.
    p. cm.
  Originally published: Decorative wrought iron work, working drawings and working notes on the making of simple, useful articles from wrought iron, brass and copper. Peoria, Ill. : Manual Arts Press, 1937.
    ISBN-13: 978-0-486-44346-1
    ISBN-10: 0-486-44346-9
    1. Ironwork. 2. Wrought-iron. I. Title.

NK8204.G6 2005
739.4—dc22

2005049241

Manufactured in the United States by RR Donnelley
44346904   2016
www.doverpublications.com

PREFACE

The purpose of this book is to give to amateur craftsmen and students some of the results of a long experience in working in metals—especially in iron and steel. It is believed that this can be done best by providing them with working drawings of small articles of use and a few notes on construction. The articles included in this collection have been selected from a much larger number because of their simplicity, because they illustrate principles, and because they represent a type of design that the author believes to be especially appropriate in the materials used. There has been no attempt to write a textbook on the theory and practice of the blacksmith's art, except in so far as pertains to the particular types of work involved in making the articles represented in the drawings. It has been assumed that the worker who uses the book will have had previous experience in at least a few of the more common and basic processes employed in forging metals.

While most of the equipment required for the work presented is in common use, a few simple tools should be added. These, however, should be made by the worker himself and, to assist him, the first part of the book is devoted to the construction of such tools. After all, the forge and the human hands are about all the tools needed.

Quite a number of the articles suggested for making involve the use of brass with iron, or of iron combined with copper. In the opinion of the author, bright iron combined with brass makes a beautiful combination; it gives sparkle, movement, and life to the work. Copper, also, combines beautifully with iron, and may be forged while hot. The heads of copper and brass rivets combine well with iron, and often add beauty to the work.

It is the hope of the author that the study and working out of these problems will stimulate the imaginations of workers and lead to a further study of design and to the creation of more things of beauty.

CONTENTS

Part I. Tools.

The tools described on the following pages are intended to supplement and not to take the place of the usual outfit of tools that constitutes a blacksmith's equipment. They are additional tools needed in making the objects described later in the book.

Fig. 1. Rivet Set

Rivet Set. One should have several rivet sets of different sizes, Fig. 1. They should be made from ⅜″, ½″, and ⅝″ octagonal tool steel. They should be made in pairs—one long and one short—the long to fasten in a vise to hold the head of the rivet, and the short one to use in making the head on the other end of the rivet.

There should be larger rivet sets made with holes or eyes punched through them for a wooden handle. This kind of rivet set is used on large hot rivets. When one has use for a rivet set, it should be made and there should be a place in which to keep it with others.

To make the depression at the end of a rivet set, the end is heated and caught vertical in a vise. A punch is ground and filed smooth on the end to the shape of a rivet head. With this punch, a depression is hammered into the hot end of the steel to be used for the set. When the depression is completed, the sides of the set are ground within 1/16″ of the depression. The set is hardened and tempered in the same manner as a chisel. See page 19.

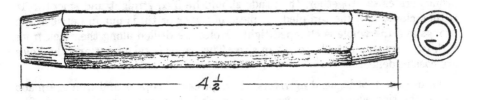

Fig. 2. Steel Stamp

Steel Stamp. Fig. 2 shows a drawing for a steel stamp that may be used to stamp hot iron with the worker's initials. The stamp is made from ½″

octagonal tool steel, 85-point carbon. To make the stamp is a very simple job. Cut the piece 4½″ long and round up each end. Grind one end flat; then file it smooth. It is reheated and allowed to anneal. With a sharp red pencil, the initial is sketched on the end in reverse.

The letter is cut into the steel with a very narrow chasing chisel. When the letter is cut lightly and correct in shape, it is gone over with a blunter chisel until the line is quite heavy. It should be tested as one proceeds. Do this by hammering it into lead. When it is finished, the edges are made a little round. Then it is hardened and tempered.

When using, the stamp is held with a pair of tongs and struck with a hammer while the metal is hot. File a straight line across the stock to enable one to know when the letter is right-side up.

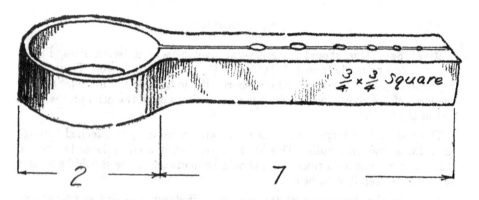

Fig. 3. Vise Heading Tool

Vise Heading Tool for Rivets. Fig. 3 shows a rivet-heading tool to be used in the vise. The stock is ¾″ square soft steel. The center of the bar is drawn flat; the stock should be made as wide as possible and about $\frac{3}{16}$″ thick. The center is to be formed into a ring as shown on the drawing. Before the prongs are closed together, the inside should be filed straight and smooth. It is then closed and the top filed. A piece of paper or tin is put in between the prongs and the whole is clamped tight. Holes are drilled along the crack from $\frac{3}{32}$″, for very small stock, to ¼″ in size. The paper is taken out and the holes are casehardened.

To use the tool in heading rivets, short pieces of copper and iron are made round the size wanted. A piece of the stock is then put into the hole it fits. The tool is fastened in the vise. The end of the rivet bar is filed flat on the top, the right amount of stock being allowed for the head to project upward. With the hammer and rivet set, the head is made. It is well to make the ends of the prongs open a little to give the tool spring. The rivets when headed will come out more freely. The spring in the tool comes from the loop or eye.

Line Gauge. In chasing lines on the surface of metal with small chisels and other tools, it is important to make a drawing with pencil or scratch awl; then go over the lines with the chasing tools.

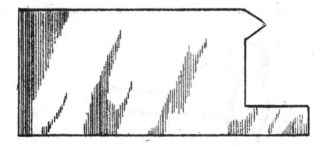

Fig. 4. Line Gauge

Fig. 4 shows a gauge for the purpose of marking lines on the edges of straight or curved forms. The guard is held against the edges, and moved along, scratching the line. The line can be made quite deep and be easy to follow with the chasing tool when cutting. The gauge can be made from a clock spring or any thin metal. There should be several sizes of the gauge.

Fig. 5. Surface Plate

Surface Plate. Fig. 5 shows a surface plate mounted on a wooden trestle. The plate is 18″ x 28″, made from cast iron, and is 3″ deep. The underside is ribbed to lighten and strengthen it. The top is machined smooth. A surface plate is used to level work upon, and for a drafting board. Work can be layed out to the correct size with chalk marks on this plate and the iron fitted to the chalk marks. In a shop there should be small surface plates 12″ x 12″ for benchwork. They are very convenient. A surface plate 3″ thick, cast without ribs, is very useful in hammering heavy pieces to straighten them.

Elm Block. When sheet metal is beaten up from one side to shape an ornament, it is called repoussé. We shall call it **bumping up** ornament on sheet metal.

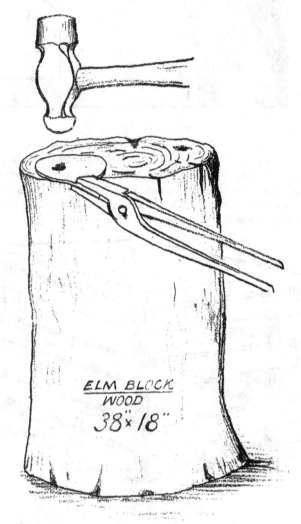

ELM BLOCK
WOOD
38″× 18″

Fig. 6. Elm Block

Fig. 6 shows an elm wood block on which to bump metal. Elm is the best wood for this purpose. The block should be about 38″ high and any diameter. Leaf forms or any kind of raised ornament are roughly raised on the elm block.

To do this, the metal is heated and, with a ball hammer of the proper size,

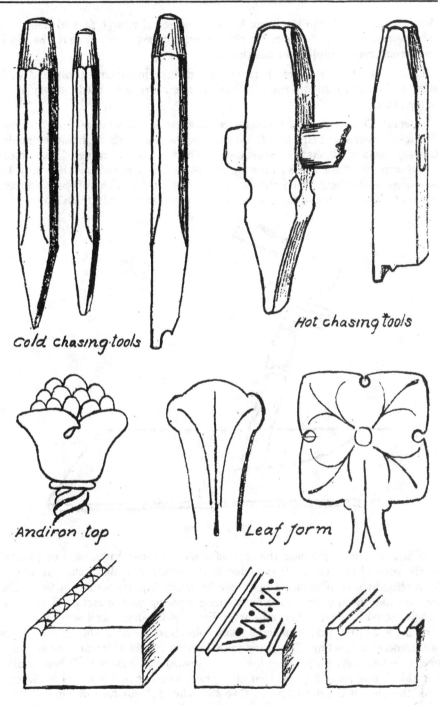

Cold chasing tools

Hot chasing tools

Andiron top

Leaf form

PLATE 1

the metal is forced into the block by hammering. If a large part of the metal is to be raised in dome shape, the sheet should be set over a hole in the block and hammered carefully to raise the metal.

Details on the metal are sharpened by hammering them up on lead with steel tools. Steel round rings of various sizes are also used on which to bump metal.

Special Tools. Special tools are required to do decorative work in iron. When one needs an extra tool to do some particular work, it should be made. Chasing tools of all shapes are required. The drawings of some of these tools are shown on Plate 1, also drawings of some line decorations that may be produced with them. One should make many tools with different shapes. Some of the tools should have a gauge or projection to guide them.

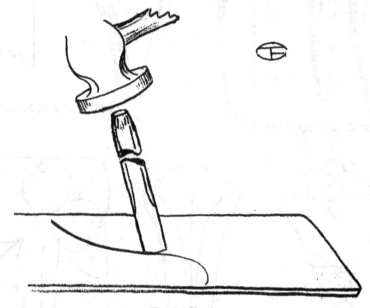

Fig. 7. Chasing

When chasing a line near the edge of a piece of metal it should be parallel to the edge of the metal. If the edge of the metal is straight, the line should be a straight line. Cutting a light line by hand requires some practice. The method used is to follow a carefully made drawing on the metal. A red lead pencil should be used to lay out curved lines, and a sharp steel scratch awl for straight lines. In chasing, a small short cold chisel is used. One of its corners is hammered into a line, Fig. 7, and then, leading the chisel toward the worker's eye, it is hammered lightly with a small broad-faced hammer. When leading the chisel, one must be sure that the forward corner of the chisel is directly over the line on the drawing. In this way, the tool can turn on curved lines. Also, one must watch the tool's forward point and not the hammer. After a

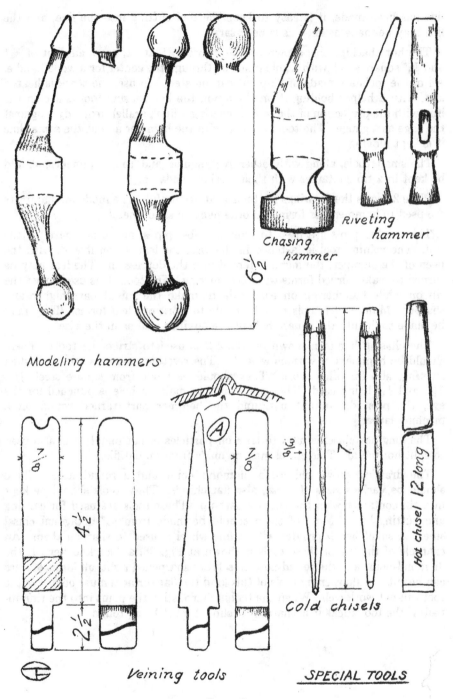

Modeling hammers

Chasing hammer

Riveting hammer

Veining tools

Cold chisels

SPECIAL TOOLS

Hot chisel 12 long

PLATE 2

line has been made, it is easy to keep the tool cutting into the line, and the line may be made as deep as is necessary.

The hot chasing tools shown on the drawing, Plate 1, are made out of ¾″ and ⅞″ square stock with a hole punched through the center for a wood handle. All of the tools are made of 85-point carbon steel. In use, the stock is heated and, with a helper holding it on the anvil, the hot chasing tool is set on the iron with the projection of the tool (if chasing a line parallel to an edge) against the edge as a gauge. The tool is struck with the hammer and at the same time it is kept moving.

The small tools, along with other rectangular and round punches, should be kept in a tin container with their working ends up.

Plate 2 shows the drawings for tools that are useful. The modeling hammers are used to hammer leaf form and ornament on sheet metal.

The veining tools are used to hammer ribs, pipes, and other parts of the leaf. The veining tool is fastened in the vise, the leaf set on it and, with the peen of the hammer, the metal is forced into the depression. The leaf may be turned to make curved forms while hammering. The tool, A, is used to set the rib on while hammering on each side to make the raised part higher and sharper. Many other tools may be made to work out leaf forms. They may be made to fit into the square hole of the anvil as well as in the vise.

The chasing hammer shown on Plate 2 is used to strike the tools. There should be hammers of various weights. The riveting hammers are used when riveting, also for other work. They should be made from square steel, ½″, ⅝″, and ¾″ being used. They are simple to make; a hole is punched for the eye, the peen drawn out flat, and the hammer part turned round on a machine lathe.

The long hot chisel is used to trim off particles of hot metal; it is also used to split hot metal. This chisel may be made from an old file.

The drawing shows chisels, a diamond point and a round nose. There should be various sizes of these, also flat chisels. These tools should be kept in a tin container with the cutting part up. These tools are used for carving and cutting lines. Most of them should be made from ⅜″ octagonal chisel steel. A small bench grinder with a fine wheel is used to sharpen them. An example of the use of these tools is shown at Fig. 38, a door knocker. If the diamond-point and the round-nose chisels are sharpened right, all kinds of lines can be cut. In sharpening tools of this kind the flat surfaces must be flat or the tool will not work well. When the tool is sharp, stick the point into the thumbnail; if the tool sticks it is sharp, if it slips it must be reground.

Part II. Notes and Cautions

The following simple notes on forge work will be of value to the beginner. To those who have had experience, they are not new. They are the outgrowth of notes made while working in metal and while teaching.

Hammering. The proper way to hold the hand hammer in forging is to catch the handle with the four fingers around it and the thumb projecting along the side and near the top part of the handle.

Hammering Iron. In drawing out iron or steel on the anvil, the piece should be placed across the anvil when receiving the blows, or at a right angle to the long way of the anvil. If the piece is hammered when it is diagonal with the long way of the anvil it will twist out of shape.

Using Tongs. When forging pieces that must be handled with tongs, always see that the tongs fit the piece nicely and, when convenient, a ring should be put on the end of reins to hold them. Do not put tongs in water while red hot, as this destroys the metal.

Flatting. Flatters and tools that are to be struck with a sledge hammer should not be used to draw iron except when absolutely necessary. The stock should be drawn out with hammer and sledge; use flatters and other tools to smooth with only.

Welding. In welding iron or steel, the fire should be thoroughly cleaned and plenty of well-burned coke used. Fresh coal should never come in contact with the parts to be united. The fire should never be allowed to spread and break out around the edges. It should be confined to the center. Coal, before it is put on fire, must be thoroughly wet. Never put wet coal on top of fire, but place it around the edges and gradually bring it to the center.

Flux. Iron and soft steel may be welded by using clean, white sand as a flux. Marble, heated red and cooled, may be pulverized and used as a flux. It should be put on just as the metal begins to take the welding heat. Borax and welding compound, also, are used for welding steel. Borax is used in brazing copper and iron.

Hardening Steel in Water. When water is used as a quenching bath for hardening steel, it should be heated just a little before the steel is cooled. Cooling steel in cold water will often cause it to check. Enough salt should be put into the water to make a strong brine bath for hardening.

Casehardening. The surface of wrought iron or soft steel can be carbonized and then made hard by heating and cooling in water. A simple way to caseharden is to heat the piece to be hardened, then roll or sprinkle it with cyanide of potassium, reheat and cool in water to harden. *Cyanide and its fumes are poisonous.*

Brazing Iron and Steel, also Copper. Iron and steel can be fastened together by brazing. In doing this, the ends are tapered or dovetailed together and bound with wire or a rivet to hold them in position. They are then placed in the fire and brought to a red heat. Some borax and spelter are put on and the heat is raised until the brass flows. The work is then taken out of the fire and let cool, then it is finished with a file or by grinding. Spelter is an alloy of copper and zinc, and may be purchased from dealers. Brass wire may also be used in brazing, and sometimes copper.

Copper may be brazed with spelter or silver solder in the same manner as iron. One should have a clean fire, well burned out—no smoke or green coal. Copper will stand considerable heat before it will melt, but not so much as iron. When the spelter flows, the work must be removed from the fire.

Welding Rings. In welding rings from flat, round, or square stock, the method used in determining the length to cut the piece is to find the inside diameter, then add the thickness of the stock used, and multiply by 3.1416, or $3\frac{1}{7}$. To this amount is added the amount of stock used to make the weld. For example, a ring is required $1''$ in thickness and its inside measure is ten inches: Solution — $10 \times 1 \times 3\frac{1}{7} = 11 \times 3\frac{1}{7} = 34\frac{1}{7}$. Add to this length enough stock to make the lap and weld. The amount needed depends on how well one can weld. Perhaps $\frac{1}{2}''$ longer is enough.

Tempering Springs. When the spring is made, it is held with a light pair of tongs. If it is very small, it is best to twist some wire around it; then catch the wire with the tongs. It is heated to a dark red and dipped into sperm oil, or equal parts of lard and tallow. When cool, it is held over the flame of the fire until the surplus oil blazes and burns off. This is repeated two or three times and allowed to cool off on a dry place on the forge.

Scratch Awl or Scriber. A scratch awl is a long piece of light, round, or square tool steel, with a tapering end. On the other end, a ring is made so it can be handled, also to hang it by. The tapered end should be hardened and tempered. A scratch awl is used to mark through a hole in metal onto another piece of metal where a hole is to be drilled, also to mark on the surface of metal.

Annealing Steel. The method of annealing steel is first to heat the piece to a red heat. It is then covered with warm, slacked lime so that the air will not come in contact with it until cool. A simple way to anneal, when in a hurry, is to heat the steel red and set it in a dry place on the forge until black. It is then plunged into water quickly and brought out. This operation is repeated until the piece is cool. Steel is also annealed by heating the piece red and setting it on the forge until cool. The slower steel is cooled, the softer it becomes. Wrought iron and mild steel forgings should always be annealed when used in work where there is danger of breaking. This relieves the strains due to forging.

Center Punch. A center punch is used to mark metal where it is to have a hole drilled, or at the point where it is to be bent. It is made from chisel steel. Small center punches are made from $\frac{5}{16}''$, $\frac{3}{8}''$, $\frac{1}{2}''$, and $\frac{5}{8}''$ octagonal stock of 80-point carbon steel. One end of the steel is drawn out tapering and round. It is ground to a very short bevel and given a sharp point. It is then hardened and tempered.

Hardening and Tempering. To harden and temper chasing tools, cold chisels, and other tools of this kind, after the tool is forged and before it is hardened, anneal it. Every forged tool should be annealed before hardening to relieve the strain due to forging.

To harden, heat to a dark red, cool the end in water, leaving the heat above the watermark. Brighten the steel with an emery stick or sandpaper. The heat in the tool will move toward the point or cutting edge. In doing so, temper color will appear on the bright part of the tool. These colors range from a pale straw to a very dark blue. The straw color indicates very hard; dark blue, quite soft. When the blue comes to the point of the tool, cool in water. The tool is now ready for use. The steel should be chisel steel, 80- or 85-point carbon. Never harden the top of a tool; that is to be struck with the hammer. The reason for not hardening this end is that, due to its hardness, particles of steel might fly and injure the worker.

Iron Lacquer. To make a liquid coating for covering iron and steel to prevent rust, a high-grade varnish is used. Cheap varnish will turn yellow and spoil the appearance of the work. The coating should dry flat.

The lacquer should be thin; if it is not, put in some more turpentine. If it does not dry flat, pour in some more wax.

It is applied to the bright iron with a soft cotton cloth or brush. This lacquer may be used on brass and copper also, if they are combined with iron.

Tool Steel. To the steel maker, temper means the percentage of carbon in steel. The word "point" means $\frac{1}{100}$ of one per cent; thus 80 point means $\frac{80}{100}$ of one per cent. Steel less than 40-point does not harden to advantage. One hundred and fifty point is $1\frac{1}{2}$ per cent. This is as high as steel is generally made.

Part III. Problems.
Votive Light No. 1

It is a custom in many churches to have lighted candles, especially in Catholic and Episcopal churches. Symbolically, the burning of candles in Catholic churches brings Jesus Christ, "the Light of the world," before the people.

The votive light in the home has come into use. It makes a very attractive, soft light that the whole family can enjoy, especially in the winter time. A

Fig. 8. Votive Light

holder for a votive light, Fig. 8, may be made of iron or copper. The glass container and the candle may be purchased at any ten-cent store.

At *A*, Plate 3, is a drawing of the frame of the holder; *B* is the glass cup that fits into the frame. The glass cup holds the candle when in use. The frame consists of the iron cup holder and four iron legs.

The construction of these iron parts is not difficult. As the glass cup is a little tapering, the cup holder must taper to correspond with it. A good way to make the cup holder is to develop a paper pattern and work from that. However, it is not difficult to make a freehand drawing of the pattern on the metal, *C*, and cut out the shape with a cold chisel. For the cup holder, the stock should be No. 16 mild steel. Notice that the pattern is ¼″ wider than the height of the finished cup holder. Heat and bend this piece of metal into the required shape. Cut the ends so that they will lap about ³⁄₁₆″. Do not scarf, but reheat and place some welding compound between the lapped ends, and then weld; or the ends may be filed straight, butted together, wired, and brazed with brass. The piece is then trued up round while cold. The best way to do this is to place it on a piece of round iron held in a vise, as shown at *D*. It is then ground and filed on each end until it is 1¼″ long. It may be decorated in any way that seems fit, or it may be left plain. The glass cup will fit better if the top and bottom of the cup holder are crimped a little so that the bearing is at the top and bottom only. See *D*.

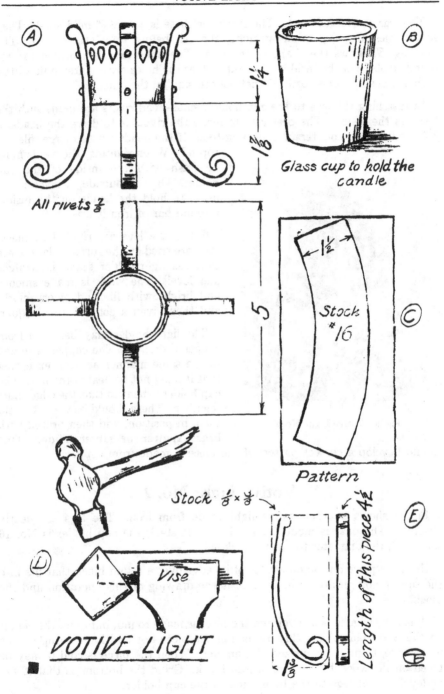

Ⓐ

All rivets ⅞

Ⓑ

Glass cup to hold the candle

Ⓒ

1½

Stock #16

5

Pattern

Stock ⅛ × ⅛

Ⓓ

Vise

Ⓔ

Length of this piece 4½

1⅜

VOTIVE LIGHT

PLATE 3

The legs are forged next. The stock for these is ⅛″ x ⅜″ mild steel. They should measure 4½″ while straight; that is, before they are formed. The drawing, *E*, shows the shape of the legs. The holes are then drilled for ⅛″ round rivets. On the inside of the cup holder the holes are countersunk a little with a brace and twist drill; do not countersink on the outside.

In fastening the legs to the cup holder, small-head rivets are used, with the head on the inside. The best way to make the rivets is to drive the heads of ⅛″ rivets into a countersunk heading tool. If the heads are too large, file the top off. When riveting, the heads must be flush with the inside of the cup holder. On the outside, a rivet set is used; to hold the heads on the inside, a round bar of iron is used.

When the legs are riveted in place' they are tried on the surface plate to see that the light-holder stand is straight and level. The work is made smooth and bright with file and emery cloth; and then given a coat of iron lacquer.

The light holder may be made from copper if desired. The copper is forged in the same manner as iron, excepting that it must not be heated too hot. The cup holder is bent so that the edges butt together. These should be wired to hold them in position, and then brazed with brass spelter or silver solder. One should develop a correct pattern if the piece is made from copper.

Fig. 9. Votive Light No. 2

Votive Light No. 2

Fig. 9 shows another votive light made from iron. The legs are nearly straight. The base is made from No. 18 soft steel; the cup holder is No. 16 soft steel; the diameter to cut the disk is 5″.

Heat the piece and hammer ⅜″ of its edge over a round block that fits into the square hole in an anvil. Fig. 10 is the drawing of this operation and the block.

When the edge is bent over and the piece is made round, bump up the center on the wood block. Do this by having the piece hot and hammering on the under side, using a large-size ball hammer. When the piece is cold it may be trued on the wood block or on a lead block. Grind the bottom so that it will be level. Rivet legs to the base, then to the cup holder.

A design may be sketched on top and cut out with drills, chisels, and files;

this makes the base more delicate. When riveting the legs to the base, file a shoulder on them so that the base will come against the shoulder. When riveting any pieces of this kind, always file the ends flat before riveting, and do not allow too much stock. If they are too long, one cannot make the joints tight.

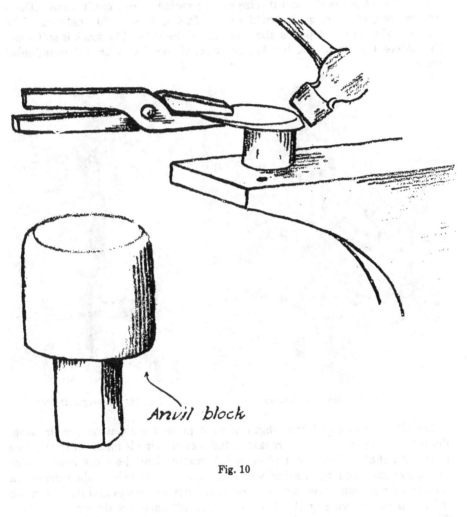

Anvil block

Fig. 10

Flowerpot Holders

Fig. 11 shows a bracket to hold two flowerpots. The pots should be decorated and glazed pots. The clay pots with the vines are to go into the glazed ones. The bracket is to be placed in the sun room or any convenient place.

The bracket is simple, and its size can be varied to suit one's needs. There are two projecting rings fastened to the frame; these hold the pots. The diameter of the rings depends upon the size of the pots. The stock is soft steel. The different parts of the bracket are riveted together with ⅛″ round-head rivets.

Fig. 11. Flowerpot Holder

Fig. 12. Flowerpot Holder

The size of stock and the length of each piece are given on the drawing, Plate 4. In constructing the bracket, a full-size drawing is made on the surface plate with chalk. The center piece is ⅜″ square. Cut the piece long enough to enlarge each end by heating and upsetting. A ¼″ hole is then drilled in each end for a round-head screw. One of the outside pieces and its length are shown on the drawing at A. The 11½″ and 12″ parts are drawn to a taper. The scrolls at the ends are formed by bending over the horn of the anvil. The drawing of the inner scroll and the length to cut the stock are shown on the drawing at B.

The arms, or parts to hold the pots, are made from one piece—from stock ½″ x ⅛″. All of the pieces are formed to fit the drawing on the surface plate, the holes drilled, and the parts riveted together with ⅛″ rivets, using rivet set in the vise on which to place the head of the rivet while riveting the other

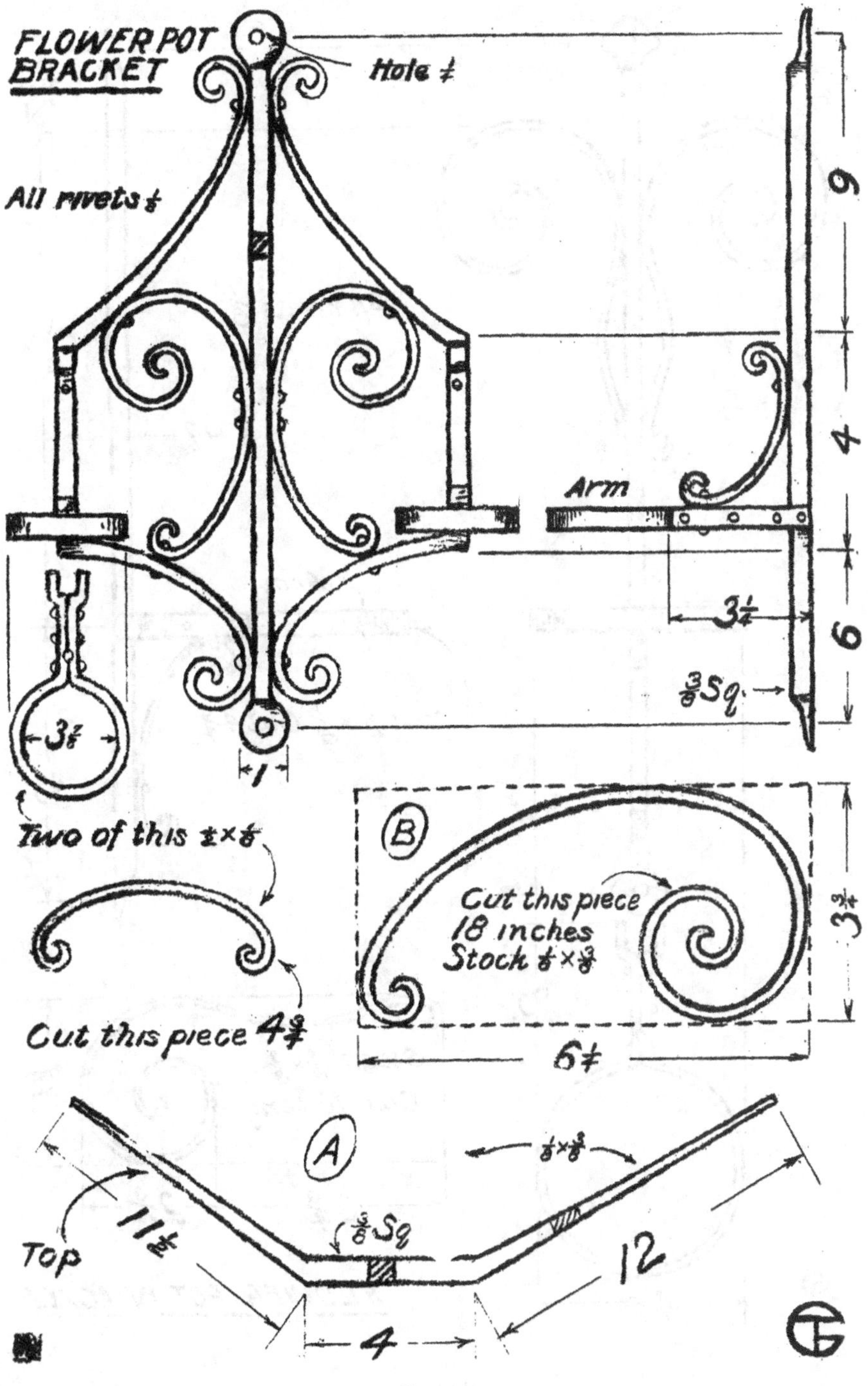
FLOWER POT BRACKET
Hole 1/4
All rivets 1/8
9
4
6
Arm
3 1/4
3/8 Sq.
3 7/8
1
Two of this 1/4 × 1/8
Cut this piece 4 3/4
B
Cut this piece
18 inches
Stock 1/8 × 3/8
3 3/4
6 1/4
A
1/8 × 3/8
Top
11 1/2
3/8 Sq
12
4

PLATE 4

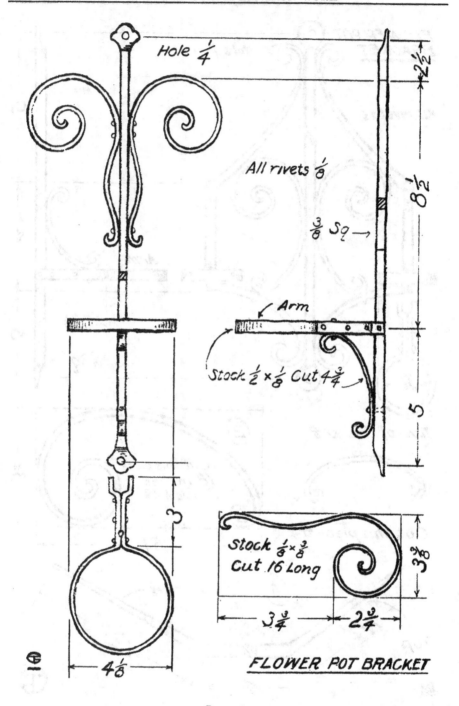

Hole $\frac{1}{4}$

All rivets $\frac{1}{8}$

$\frac{3}{8}$ Sq →

Arm

Stock $\frac{1}{2} \times \frac{1}{8}$ Cut $4\frac{3}{4}$

$2\frac{1}{2}$

$8\frac{1}{2}$

5

3

$4\frac{1}{8}$

Stock $\frac{1}{8} \times \frac{3}{8}$
Cut 16 Long

$3\frac{3}{8}$

$3\frac{3}{4}$ $2\frac{3}{4}$

FLOWER POT BRACKET

PLATE 5

end. When the whole bracket is riveted, emery cloth is used to brighten it. Then give the whole a coat of iron lacquer.

Fig. 12 is a single flower bracket and Plate 5 is a drawing of it. This bracket is made in the same manner as explained for the construction of the double bracket. The bracket may be used in garden summer houses, or on each side of the entrance door of the home, to hold glazed pots with vines. The flower brackets should have at least two coats of iron lacquer.

Flower Stand

The stand, Fig. 13, consists of the center handle, the two containers to hold the pots, the arms, and the base. It is made from soft steel. The containers are made from No. 20 sheet steel. The disk for each of these is cut 5¾" in

Fig. 13. Flower Stand

diameter. The process of making is as follows: Heat the disk. Set it on the end of a piece of 4" steam pipe placed on the anvil. Plate 6, A. On the disk, set a piece of 3" steam pipe. On this piece of 3" pipe, place a piece of flat iron. Strike this iron with a hammer until the disk is driven into the 4" pipe, reheating the disk in the process. The pipes should be smooth, without any sharp edges, so as not to cut the disks. Flat iron rings welded, also, could be used to raise the sides. The drawing of the raised container is shown at Fig. 14.

The wrinkles of the container are heated and hammered out on the anvil. This is done by hammering on the inside with a light riveting hammer. The corner is sharpened by hammering it on an anvil block. When the container is shaped and is true, the scallops at the top are cut with a chisel and filed; the holes are drilled, including the hole in the center of the container; this hole is squared to fit the tenon on the arm. The center of the container is bumped down so that the riveting of the arm will not interfere with the clay drip pan or glazed pot when that is in place. The bumping is done by hammering the pieces on the wood block while cold.

The stock for the arms is ⅜" square soft steel. There is a ⁵⁄₁₆" square tenon filed on one end. The other end of the bar is drawn out tapering, and the length of the piece when finished is 19½" from the shoulder of the tenon to the other

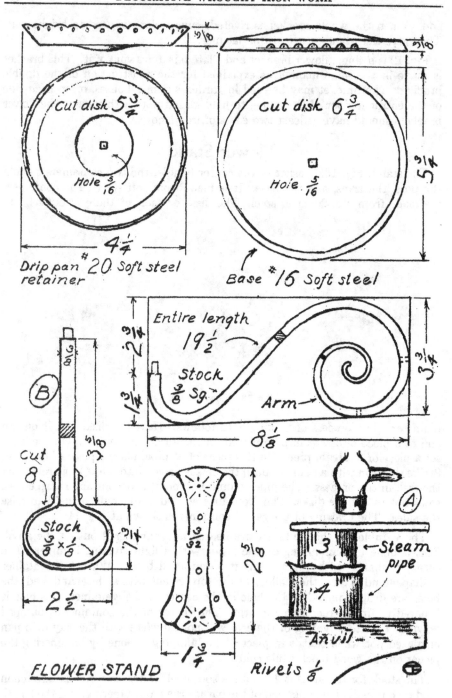

Cut disk $5\frac{3}{4}$

Hole $\frac{5}{16}$

$\frac{5}{8}$

Drip pan #20 Soft steel retainer

$4\frac{1}{4}$

cut disk $6\frac{3}{4}$

Hole $\frac{5}{16}$

$\frac{3}{8}$

$5\frac{3}{4}$

Base #16 Soft steel

Entire length $19\frac{1}{2}$

Stock $\frac{3}{8}$ Sg.

Arm →

$2\frac{3}{4}$

$1\frac{3}{4}$

$3\frac{3}{4}$

$8\frac{1}{8}$

B

$\frac{3}{8}$

cut 8

$3\frac{5}{8}$

Stock $\frac{3}{8} \times \frac{1}{8}$

$7\frac{3}{4}$

$2\frac{1}{2}$

$\frac{3}{32}$

$2\frac{5}{8}$

$1\frac{3}{4}$

FLOWER STAND

A

3

← Steam pipe

4

Anvil

Rivets $\frac{1}{8}$

PLATE 6

end. When bending the scroll it must not be heated too hot and must fit the chalk drawing previously made on the iron surface plate.

The base is made from No. 16 soft sheet steel. If this size is not available, it can be drawn out from a thicker piece. The edge is heated and hammered over an anvil block or on the end of a large bar of iron fastened in a vise. The piece is trued when cool, and the center is bumped up. The base is set on the surface plate, and the bottom trimmed with a cold chisel. Then it is ground or filed to make it level. A $\frac{5}{16}''$ square hole is made in the center through which to fasten the handle E by riveting.

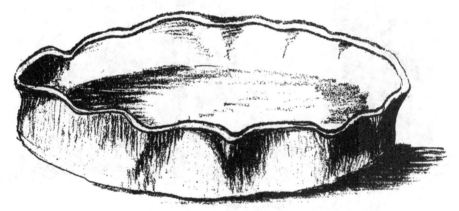

Fig. 14. Flower Container

The handle is made next. The loop at the top is made and riveted to the upright with $\frac{1}{8}''$ round-head rivets, rivet sets on both ends of the rivet being used. In riveting the handle to the base, the handle is fastened in the vise and the base set on it and riveted. The base is set on the surface plate to see that the handle stands vertical.

The arms are riveted to the handle, and set onto the surface plate to see that the outer ends of the arms touch the plate. The center decorated plate is made from $\frac{3}{32}''$ thick stock. The outline is sketched on the metal, and the plate cut out with a cold chisel, then filed on the edges. The line ornament on the plate is done with a chasing chisel. The plate is drilled, also the scrolls and handle. The whole is riveted together. The containers are riveted in place, and the work tried on the surface plate to see that it is straight. The whole work is smoothed with file and emery cloth. It is then lacquered.

A flower stand similar to the one shown in Fig. 13 may be made from much lighter stock, if one desires, and very much smaller in size. The center base and the containers at the ends may be made from No. 20 gauge copper. The arms may be made from one piece of soft steel $\frac{3}{8}''$ x $\frac{1}{8}''$, with a loop in the center to be used as a handle. The arms may be riveted to the base with $\frac{1}{8}''$ round-head rivets. The ends of the arms may be formed into a volute scroll with the containers riveted at the top. The whole stand may be very simple.

Table Ash Trays

Fig. 15 shows a nest of ash trays. The rack will hold twelve trays. They can be easily moved, as the volute scroll serves for a handle. These trays are to be used on the table and at bridge parties.

The rack consists of four parts: the base, the handle, and the two forward uprights. The handle and the uprights are also the guards that keep the trays from falling out. The base and trays are made from 20-gauge, soft steel. The guard and handle are soft.

Fig. 15. Table Ash Trays

The illustration shows, too, a picture of a cast-iron die. The metal is hammered into the die to make the base of the rack and the trays; the depression is ⅜″ deep. The die can be made on any machine lathe from a flat, cast-iron block.

The drawing for each part is shown in Plate 7. The base, A, is made by cutting a square piece of No. 20 gauge steel a little larger than the dimensions on the drawing. The die is set on a large block of wood and, after heating, the sheet of steel is hammered into the die with a hammer and a hickory mallet, B. When the sheet fits the depression, it is reheated, and the small depressions on the rim are made by driving a piece of ⅜″ round iron into them. Make a depression on one side, reheat, and make the other. The depressions in the die should be about ⁷⁄₁₆″ wide; the depth should be quite shallow.

The base is layed out as shown by the drawing, a pair of dividers and a red lead pencil being used. Then cut the pattern out with a cold chisel. File or grind the edges. Fasten a piece of iron vertically in a vise, having one side rounded and the end flat. About ¼″ of the edge and also the feet of the base are hammered to a right angle. While doing this, the edge must be kept hot. When cold, the legs are turned up a little and leveled on a surface plate.

The trays are also heated, hammered into the die, and cut out to the size shown on the drawing. The rims may be decorated, lines being cut with a small, blunt cold chisel and punches.

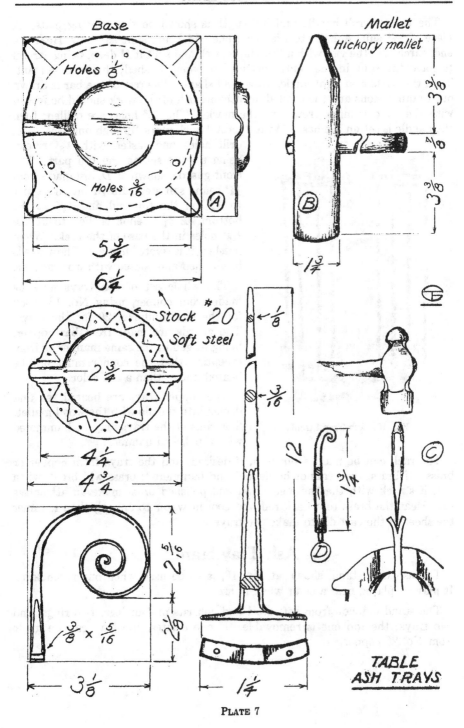

PLATE 7

The volute-scroll handle and its length is shown on the drawing plate. A piece of $\frac{3}{8}''$ square, soft steel is used, one end being split as at C. Heat the end, catch it in the vise with a thin, hot chisel, and split it 1" deep, being careful to have the split in the center of the bar when finished; this is important. Turn the parts at a right angle, draw, and shape. The rest of the bar is drawn out to dimensions and then rolled into shape. All of the work should be forged with the hand hammer, retaining the marks. The $\frac{1}{8}''$ holes are drilled; then the handle is set on the base. With a scratch awl, mark through onto the base; drill holes and fasten with $\frac{1}{8}''$ rivets, using a rivet set on the top part. The front guards, shown at D, are made from $\frac{1}{4}''$ round soft steel, drawn out on a taper to $\frac{1}{8}''$ on the top end and $\frac{1}{4}''$ at the bottom. A $\frac{3}{16}''$ tenon is filed to fit the $\frac{3}{16}''$ holes in the base of the rack. When finished, it is riveted in place. The whole is brightened and coated with iron lacquer.

Fig. 16. Ash Tray Stands

The whole set of ash trays may be made from copper, using No. 18 stock for the base and No. 20 for the trays. The guards are made from bar copper, being forged in the same manner as iron, excepting that the copper must not be heated hotter than a red color.

The copper trays are heated red and driven into the die with the wood mallet. The rims of the trays may be hammered with a polished hammer.

The rack can be made from iron, if desired, and the trays from copper or brass. If brass, they cannot be heated and hammered; brass will break when hot, if struck with the hammer. Iron and polished brass make an attractive set. Heat the brass to a dark red and cool in water to anneal, then hammer the sheet in the cast die to make the trays.

Ash Tray Stand

The ash tray stand, shown at Fig. 16, is to be used when one is smoking. It may be placed near a chair when in use.

The stand is made from soft steel and consists of four legs, two rings, and two trays; the top one is removable. If one desires, the tray can be made from No. 20 copper.

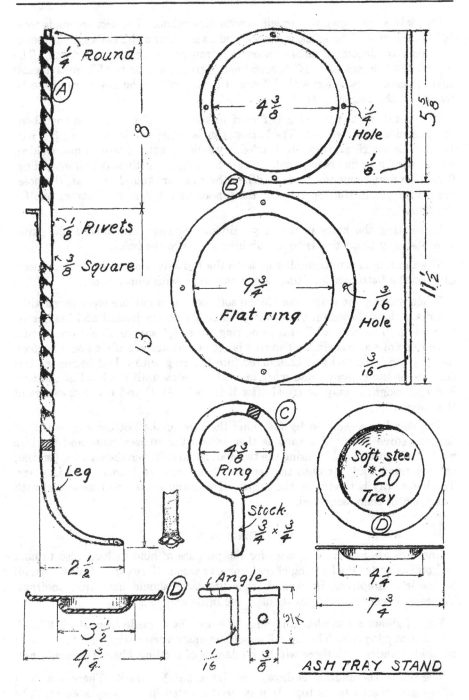

ASH TRAY STAND

PLATE 8

On Plate 8 are shown the drawings with dimensions. The legs are made from
⅜" square steel. The stock is heated and twisted, and the ends are flattened;
they may be decorated as shown on the drawing, or in any other way. The
top ends of the legs have ¼" tenons filed to rivet the ring to. There is a small
angle riveted to each leg with ⅛" round head rivets. The lower tray is to be
riveted to the angles. See A.

The metal for the top ring is forged to the size ⅝" x ⅛". It is then bent
into ring shape and welded. The bottom ring is larger and heavier — ⅞" x ³⁄₁₆".
In welding the rings, they are scarfed, without upsetting, lapped and welded,
a clean sand as a flux being used. In case the ring is a little small after welding,
it may be drawn out to the size. When the rings are round and flat, the holes
are drilled ¼" in the top ring for the tenons and ³⁄₁₆" in the bottom one for
the rivets.

In locating the holes in the rings, divide the ring into four, equal parts.
The best way to do this is to use dividers to space the holes.

The top ring is countersunk a little on the top side; the bottom one countersunk on the bottom side. Rings are shown at B, with dimensions.

When making the trays, use No. 20 soft steel, and cut the piece larger than
the dimensions shown on the drawing. The sheets are heated and hammered
into rings. The ring at C is a loose ring from ¾" square stock; one should
have rings of various sizes. The ring is set on the surface plate and the stock
for tray top is heated and hammered into the ring with a ball hammer. Use
the face of the hammer, and work around the edge until the bowl of the tray
is deep enough; it may be trued after it is cool. At D and D are drawings of
the trays.

The stand is assembled by fastening the legs to the bottom ring with ³⁄₁₆"
flathead stove bolts. The work is then set on the surface plate and the legs
made to stand vertical by using the two-foot square. When the legs are vertical,
the top ring should fit onto the tenons. The rings are then riveted in place.
The lower tray is riveted to the angles. The stand is filed and smoothed with
emery cloth; then lacquered.

Andirons

Andirons are used in fireplaces for the purpose of holding logs; also to hold
an iron basket for the burning of coal, coke, or wood. There is no fire as cheerful
as one in a fireplace. Brick and stone fireplaces should have iron andirons.
The more decorated mantles should have brass andirons.

Fig. 17 shows a complete andiron. The upright is made from stock 3" x 2"
with a heavy log rail. The log rail should be made very heavy, or a foot should
be welded under it so there will be no danger of settling when it becomes hot.

The top of the andiron is drawn out flat about ⅜" thick. There is a band
⅜" square riveted to its top. It may be decorated in any way seen fit. The
stock is soft steel.

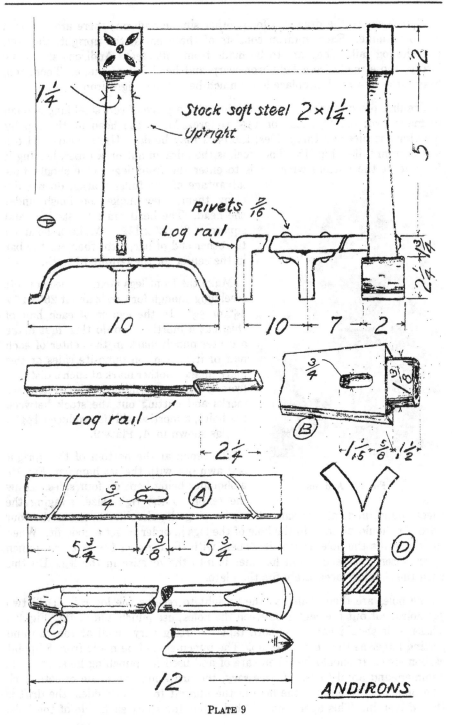

Stock soft steel $2 \times 1\frac{1}{4}$

Upright

Rivets $\frac{7}{16}$

Log rail

$1\frac{1}{4}$

2

5

$2\frac{1}{4}$ $1\frac{3}{4}$

10

10 7 2

Log rail

$\frac{3}{4}$

$\frac{3}{8}$

Ⓑ

$2\frac{1}{4}$

$1\frac{1}{15}$ $\frac{5}{8}$ $1\frac{1}{2}$

$\frac{3}{4}$ Ⓐ

$5\frac{3}{4}$ $1\frac{9}{8}$ $5\frac{3}{4}$

Ⓒ

Ⓓ

12

ANDIRONS

PLATE 9

Plate 9 shows the drawings for another simple andiron; there are two in a set, both alike. Each andiron consists of three parts: the upright, the feet, and the log rail. They are to be made from soft steel. Andirons should be heavy; those made from light iron warp and bend out of shape. Then, too, heavy iron in a brick fireplace looks much better than light iron.

The first piece to make is the upright. Cut a piece of soft steel long enough to make two; use 2" x 1¼" or 1½" square. Make the head at the top by fullering the piece on three sides; the back may be flat. Use a good-sized top and bottom fuller, Fig. 18. The stock is then drawn out on a taper, leaving it full size at the bottom where it is to enter the front legs. One should take advantage of the fuller marks; do not destroy them; they make the finish under the head. The head must be straight and square — 2" x 2" x 1¼". Make a head on the other end of bar, also; then cut the bar in the center, or the required length.

Fig. 17. Andiron

Make the front legs next. A piece of soft steel long enough for two is about 26" x 2" x ½" or ⅝". In the center of each half of this, cut a mortise. To do this, first make a center-punch mark in the center of each half of it. Then, on opposite sides of this mark; make another mark at such a distance from it that, by drilling ¾" holes at these marks and cutting out the stock between the holes, a mortise will be produced 1⅜" x ¾", as shown in A, Plate 9.

The tenon at the bottom of the upright is drawn out with the set hammer, Fig. 19, a shoulder being kept on four sides. Draw the tenon to the right size, swaging the edges round, and, at the same time, keeping the shoulder even on the four sides. It should be tried in the hole of the legs in order to get a good fit. When the tenon fits the hole, reheat it. Then, with the leg over the vise or a punch block, insert the tenon, and hammer it into the mortise in the leg. Do this until the shoulder accurately fits the plate.

The holes are then drilled in the upright to receive the log rail. Drill two ⅝" holes; cut out the center between the holes; use punch and drifts. Fig. 20. These tools should have a smooth taper, starting very small at the end and getting larger as they near the top. The punch should be made from 85-point carbon steel. It should be taken care of and used for punching holes to make hammers and anvil tools. If necessary, the drifts may be made of soft steel. The punch is driven into the hole in the upright from both sides; the drift is then driven in. This operation will bulge out the stock each side of the hole.

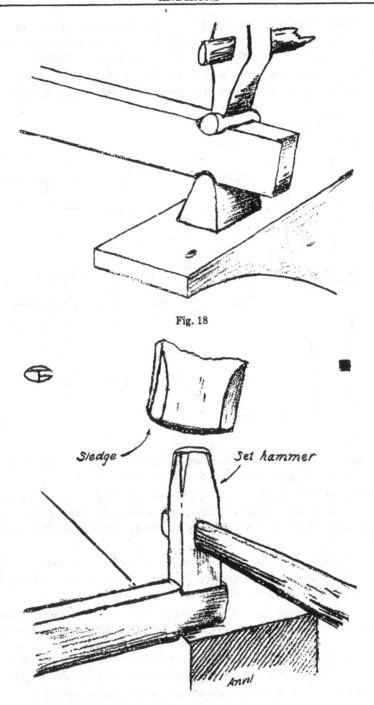

Fig. 18

Sledge

Set hammer

Anvil

Fig. 19

It is hammered back with the drift in the hole. Also insert the tenon into the hole of the leg. Hammer on the head to square up the shoulder while the drift is in the hole. See the finished drawing of the lower part of upright B, Plate 9.

The top or head is decorated with a tool shown at C. This tool is made of 85-point tool steel and can be used for other work. Heat the head, and hammer

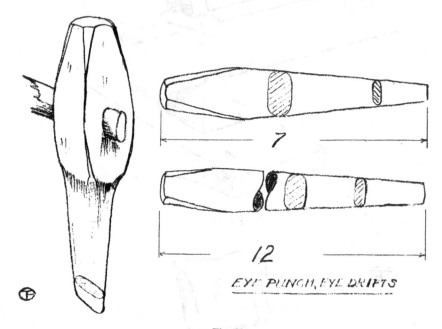

EYE PUNCH, EYE DRIFTS

Fig. 20

the cutting end into the head as shown on the drawing. The center is made with a round punch, ground round on the end instead of flat.

The whole upright is heated to a dark red and the corners are hammered. This is done to straighten up the shaft and destroy all sharp parts. Do not hammer the corners of the head. Do not hammer with the ball of the hammer to make marks.

Bend the front legs to the right; shape and hammer the corners. If the feet are long, they should be cut, making the length over all 10″. The andirons are to fit a fireplace 20″ deep. Rivet the upright in the legs.

Cut the stock for the log rail long enough to include the short center leg; then split the end of the bar with a hot chisel after the bar is fastened in the vise. See the drawing of the split end, D, Plate 9. Be sure that the split is in the center of the bar. If it is not, one side will be thinner than the other. The split parts are bent at a right angle and squared up. Cut off at the proper length.

The bar for the log rail is shouldered on two sides to make the tenon. This is done in the same manner as the upright. The other end is bent at a right angle.

The center foot is then riveted in place with $\frac{3}{16}''$ rivets. These rivets can be made from $\frac{3}{16}''$ round, soft steel, or drawn from heavier stock. A foot welded on will make a stronger job.

The log rail is then riveted into the upright. More than one heat will be necessary to work a good rivet end. Reheat the rivet end, care being taken not to get the work too hot. Hammer on the end of stock until the heat is black. Set the andiron on a surface plate and make it stand straight.

Fig. 21 shows a set of andirons with basket and fire tools. The tools are to be hung upon hooks, one on each side of the opening of the fireplace, or on the end of fireplace.

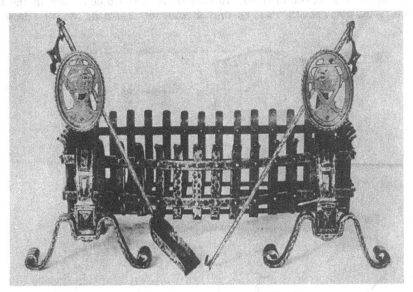

Fig. 21. Andiron, Basket, and Tools

Poker, Shovel, and Crane

A fireplace should be equipped with a poker and shovel to use around the fire. They may be hung on the front of the fireplace, or at the ends, when not in use. They will also decorate the fireplace. Iron tools are suitable for a brick or a stone fireplace. One may also use an iron rack to hold the fire tools.

Plate 10 shows drawings for a poker and a shovel. They are made from soft steel. The shovel, A, consists of three parts: the ring, the handle, and the bowl. The poker also has a ring.

Hooks are to be fastened to the fireplace with expansion bolts, or built in with the mason work to hold the tools. The stock for the bowl, B, is No. 20 gauge soft steel; it is cut out with thin cold chisels. The sheet is heated and hammered on the elm block to form the shape. Use a large ball hammer until the bowl is brought up. The sides may be hammered over the end of the anvil to bring them up. When cool, the bowl is trued and made straight; all dents are hammered out.

The handle is made from ½″ square stock; one end is upset and made round. Bend a collar from stock ⅞″ x ³⁄₁₆″ into a ring. Shape it and drive it onto the end of the handle. See that the end of the ring is not quite together, as the stock will stretch when welding. Heat the end to a white heat and dip into the sand; reheat to a welding heat and weld. When raising the heat it should not be given too much blast at the beginning; heat slowly in order to get the heat even throughout or the collar will become too hot while the handle will be cool. Welding compound may be used if one can weld better with it. The collar at the end is rounded up. In case there is too much stock in the ball, a thin, hand hot chisel is used to chip off some of the stock. See the drawings at *C*.

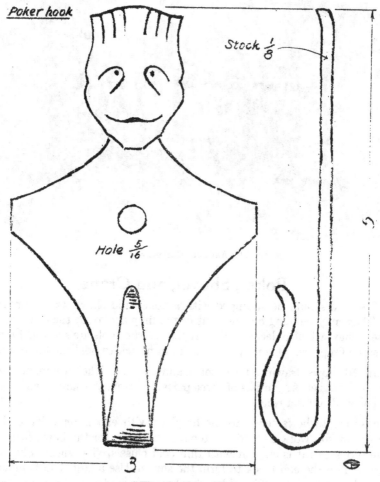

Fig. 22. Poker Hook

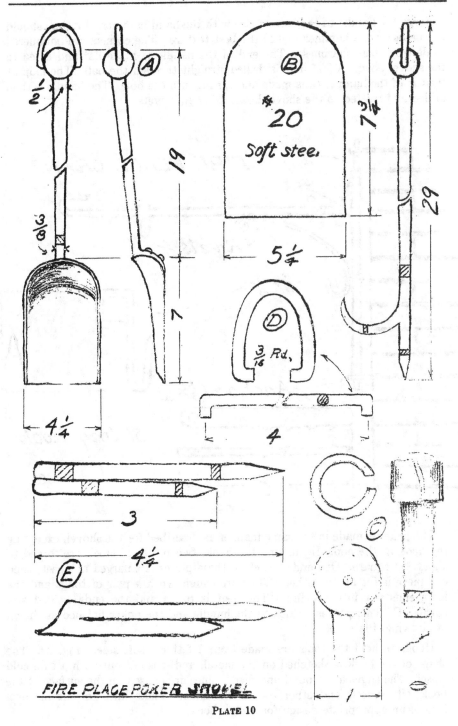

PLATE 10

Forge the handle to the correct size with the hand hammer. Flatters should not be used; the hammer makes the best texture. The corners are hammered to destroy their sharpness. The end of the handle is made flat and fitted to the shovel bowl. A $\frac{3}{16}$" hole is drilled straight through the ball. The loop at the top of the handle, *D*, is made and sprung into the hole. The handle is then drilled and riveted to the shovel bowl, using $\frac{3}{16}$" rivets.

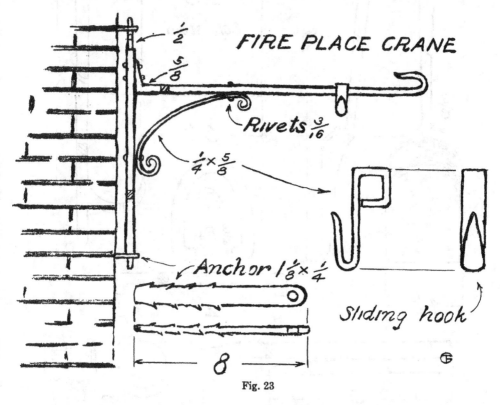

Fig. 23

The poker is made in the same manner as described for the shovel, excepting the hook at the end. In making the hook, two pieces of stock are forged to about $\frac{3}{8}$" square. One end of each of these pieces is enlarged or upset; then one piece is set on the other. They are caught with a pair of tongs and the large ends put into the fire. The heat is taken and the ends welded and scarfed, *E*. This part is welded to the handle and the poker finished as shown on drawing, Plate 10.

Hooks to hold the tools are made from $\frac{1}{8}$" thick, soft steel. Fig. 22. The shape of the hook is sketched on the metal, and it is cut out with a thin cold chisel. The edges are ground and filed. Lines are chased on the surface of the hook with chisels and other tools. One should make lines to suit his own idea of an appropriate design for such a book.

Fig. 23 shows the drawings for a crane to be built into a fireplace. In early times, the crane was used for the purpose of holding cooking pots. The crane is in use today in some places. It is also very decorative and should be used in stone and brick fireplaces.

The size to make the crane depends on the size of the opening in the fireplace. The crane should be forged with the hand hammer, drawing the stock from a larger piece. The marks that the hammer makes should be retained.

The hook on the crane should be made loose, so that it will move along the bar. It should be put onto the bar before the crane is assembled. The anchors are cut along the edge with a cold chisel, making projections that will hold in the mason work. Notice that the anchors are set so the bracket may be raised upwards, releasing the tenon in the lower anchor and making it possible to remove the crane.

Candlesticks

Candlesticks are made from all kinds of metal. Candles date back to remote ages and, all down through the ages, they have been used for light. Nowadays they are used as decorations in the home. Iron candlesticks are very suitable and decorative on the shelf of a brick or stone fireplace. They should be used in pairs, perhaps with a clock on the mantel shelf. Fig. 24.

Plate 11 shows a drawing of a candlestick which is very simple to make. It consists of four parts: the socket or retainer to hold the candle, the drip pan, the twisted upright, and the base. It is made from soft steel.

The socket, A, is made from No. 20 soft steel. The shape is sketched on the metal and cut out with a cold chisel. It is then filed on the edges and a $\frac{3}{16}''$ hole drilled in the center. It may be bent into shape while cold with a ball hammer. The center is bumped up on the elm block, bringing up the forks. The balance is simple.

Fig. 24. Candlestick

The drip pan, B, is made from soft sheet steel, No. 20 gauge. The disk is cut $4\frac{3}{4}''$ in diameter. It is then heated and bumped up over a hole on the elm block, also on a piece of lead. The scallops on the edge are filed. Their shape should be laid out with a red lead pencil and finished with a file. The raised lines on the drawings of the pan are sketched and bumped from the outside to the inside. Fasten a veining tool in the vise and, with a flat peen modeling hammer, the metal is driven into the tool. A $\frac{3}{16}''$ hole is drilled in the center.

The base is No. 18 sheet steel. The diameter is $3\frac{3}{4}''$. Catch the piece with

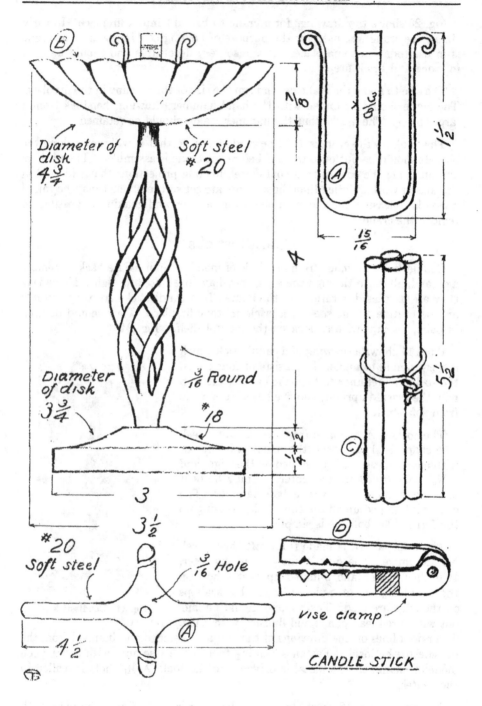

CANDLE STICK

PLATE 11

a pair of light, flat-nose tongs; then heat and bump it into a hole in the elm block until the center part is about the right height. It is then cooled and, with a pair of dividers, with one leg on the center, a line is scratched, making the diameter 3″. The edge is then heated and hammered over a round, iron block that fits the square hole of the anvil. The block should be flat on top with square edges. A large, short bar of round iron with a flat end fastened in the vise can be used for this work.

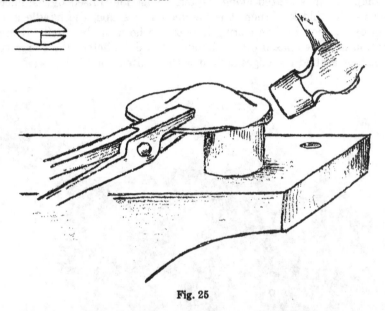

Fig. 25

The drawing of this operation is shown at Fig. 25. After the edge is hammered over, when cool, the base is trued up. Fasten a ¾″ round bar in the vise with the end up; file the end flat. Set the base on the bar directly in the center; hammer the metal flat; true up the sides again on a larger bar. Drill a ³⁄₁₆″ hole in the center, and grind the bottom so that it will be level on the surface plate.

At C on the drawing, Plate 11, are shown four ³⁄₁₆″ round rods wired together. Catch them in a round-nose pair of tongs and place a ring on one end of the reins to bind them firmly. Heat that end and, using sand as a flux, weld the ends and draw down to about ⅜″ round. The other end is welded in the same manner. The rods are then heated the entire length to an even heat. Cool one end, and catch it in a vise, twisting the whole to the left, in this case. Reheat, and twist them tighter. They are now heated again, and twisted to the right. This will swell them in the center. True the rods when cool.

On each end, a tenon is filed. The candle holder, drip pan, and base are riveted on after the tenon has been filed flat on the end and is the correct length for riveting. The end of the upright is put between the jaws of the clamp, D; the whole is then made tight in the vise and the pieces riveted on with a light riveting hammer. When the base is riveted, the candlestick is leveled and made to stand straight. Smooth with a file and emery cloth. It is then given a coat of iron lacquer.

Fig. 26 shows a reproduction of another candle holder, and Plate 12 shows the drawing of it with dimensions. The stock is soft steel. The pattern A is cut from No. 18 stock; the edges are ground or filed. To raise the stock in bowl shape, B, it is heated along the outer edge and raised by hammering it on the wooden block. When it is hammered in shape, the handle is heated and an eye turned by hammering it over the horn of the anvil. If any line decoration is to be chased on the handle, it is done before the eye is turned. The scallops around the edges are cut with a chisel, and filed.

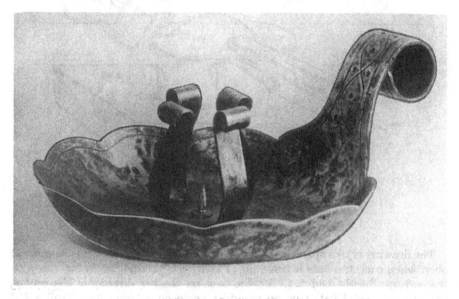

Fig. 26. Candle Holder

The socket to hold the candle is made from No. 20 soft steel. The drawing for socket and pattern is at C. When the pattern is cut out and filed on the edges, a $\frac{3}{16}''$ hole is drilled in the center to hold the spike and rivet. It is then formed into shape while the metal is cold.

The rivet with the spike on its head may be filed to the dimensions given on the drawing. The spike in the center of the socket is used to press the end of the candle on to hold it upright. To make a jig for assembling the holder, use a piece of round iron, flat on top, with a $\frac{1}{8}''$ hole drilled in the center. The other end is drawn flat so the piece may be fastened in the vise, D. To assemble the holder, the spike is set in the holder, the piece fastened in the vise, and the socket set on the rivet end of the spike; then the bowl, B, which has a $\frac{3}{16}''$ hole drilled in the center and countersunk. The two pieces are riveted. The work is filed and smoothed with emery cloth. Then it is given a coat of lacquer.

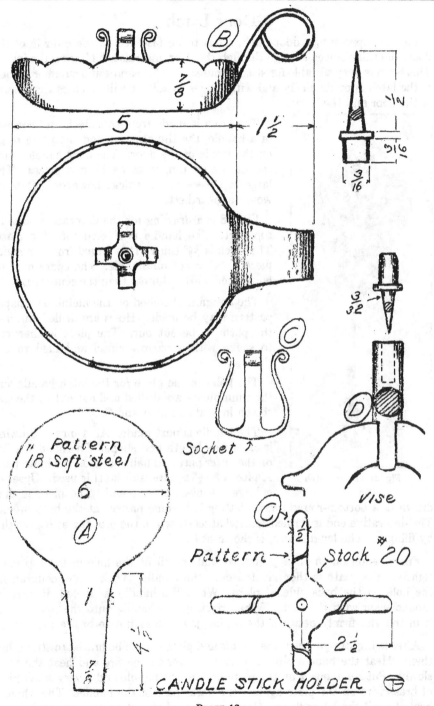

B

7/8

5

1 1/2

1/2

3/16

3/16

C

3/32

D

Socket

Vise

Pattern
18 Soft steel

6

A

C

Pattern→

1/2

Stock #20

1

4 1/2

7/8

2 1/2

CANDLE STICK HOLDER

PLATE 12

Door Latch

Fig. 27 represents a door latch. It is to be fastened to the outside of the door; the thumbpiece is to go through the door and raise the bar on the inside. This latch is very suitable for stucco houses, also for cabins and summer homes. If the latch is made nicely and with hinges to suit, it will enhance the beauty of the door and the home.

Fig. 27. Door Latch

The latch is made from soft steel, and consists of a handle, the thumbpiece, and the parts to go on the inside of the door. The door handle, with the decorated top, is made in two pieces. The large top piece is ⅛″ thick; however, ¼″ thick would appear better.

Fig. 28 is a drawing for the decorative plate or top part. The handle is riveted into the plate. The stock is ⅛″ thick. It is forged from a heavier piece if ⅛″ is not obtainable. The edges may be hammered a little thinner than the center part.

The design is sketched on the metal, or a paper pattern may be made. Holes are drilled through the parts to be cut out. The plate is then cut to shape with a narrow chisel and filed to the right size.

The holes in the plate for the latch handle and the thumbpiece are drilled and cut out to the size shown in Plate 13 at *B* and *C*.

The handle is next made. At *A* on the drawing is shown its length and shape. The handle is flat on the outer part and half round on the inner part. A piece of ½″ square, soft steel is used. Upset or enlarge the piece on one end. The piece is then drawn in a bottom-round swage, letting it become narrow at the bottom end. The decorative end is formed somewhat as shown in the drawing at *B*. Do this by filing it. The length, also, is shown at *B*.

File a tenon on the heavy end, so that it will fit the hole in the top plate tightly. The plate is then riveted onto the handle. With a file, countersink the hole on the back side of plate. When the handle is riveted, it may be ground even with the plate. When riveting the handle onto the plate, catch it in the vise firmly between the copper jaws, so as not to bruise the handle.

After being straightened, the handle and plate should be brazed to strengthen them. Heat the handle red; then turn it over in the fire and heat the plate slowly. Put some borax on the plate next to the handle and a very small piece of brass wire on the plate against the lower part of the handle. The whole is heated until the brass flows. Care must be taken not to use too much brass,

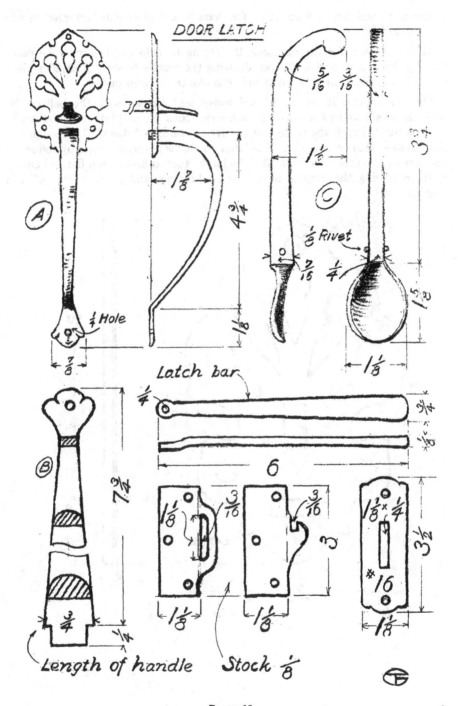

DOOR LATCH

Latch bar

6

Length of handle   Stock ⅛

PLATE 13

as the work will not look so well. The handle and plate can be forged in one piece if desired.

At *C* is shown the thumbpiece. In forging it, a large piece may be used, making the thumb part first, then drawing the handle to size. A smaller piece of stock, if used, is upset on one end to make the thumb part.

The thumbpiece is set in an oval swage and formed with the ball of the hammer, as shown by the drawing. A hole is drilled for a $\frac{1}{8}''$ rivet. The thumb-piece is put through the plate and the rivet hammered down. This keeps the thumbpiece from coming out. The latch bar is very easy to make by following the dimensions given on Plate 13. The latch is smoothed with a file and emery cloth, removing the surplus brass due to brazing, and given a coat of iron lacquer.

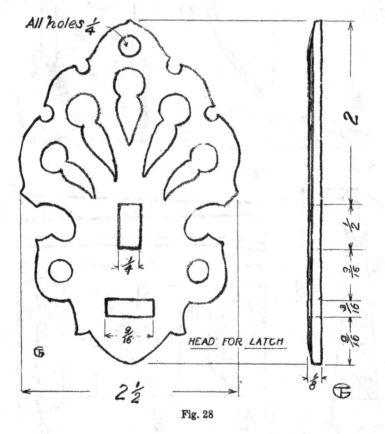

Fig. 28

Inside Door Latch

Fig. 29 shows the inside of a latch and a bar to lock the door. When the bar is not in use it hangs downward. To lock the door, the bar is pulled up and into the keeper on the doorcasing.

The drawings for each of the parts are shown on Plate 14. The stock is soft steel, and the design is in keeping with the latch shown on Plate 13. It may

be used with the outside part of that latch if desired. In making the parts of the latch, the plate at A is made from $\frac{1}{8}''$ thick stock, but should be hammered thinner from a thicker piece, using only the hand hammer, and retaining the marks made from the hammering out of the plate.

The outer part of the plate is cut to the dimensions given on the drawing. The open work at the top is sketched on the metal with a red lead pencil; $\frac{3}{8}''$ holes are drilled at the top of the open work; a $\frac{1}{4}''$ hole is drilled below; the balance is cut out with a chisel, and filed. One may drill a small hole at the bottom, if desired, and then cut out the parts between the holes.

All other holes are $\frac{7}{32}''$. The square holes are made with a square punch. Use a little oil on the punch and drift out the holes with a hand hammer. This work is punched while the metal is cold. The back of the square holes are countersunk. This is done with a brace and drill for this kind of work and retained for this use. The three top holes are countersunk for flathead screws. The other holes are for round-head screws.

Fig. 29. Inside Door Latch

The keepers, B and C, are made $\frac{1}{8}''$ thick. They are cut out with drills and cold chisels. The edges are filed, and they are countersunk for flathead screws. These holes are drilled $\frac{7}{32}''$, also. The slot in keeper B is to hold the bar. The slot is set out $\frac{1}{8}''$, the thickness of the latch on the Plate A. This will allow the bar to drop into the slot.

The guard to hold the latch bar is at D. The stock is drawn from a heavier bar, and formed as shown by the drawing. The tenons are $\frac{1}{4}''$ square. These

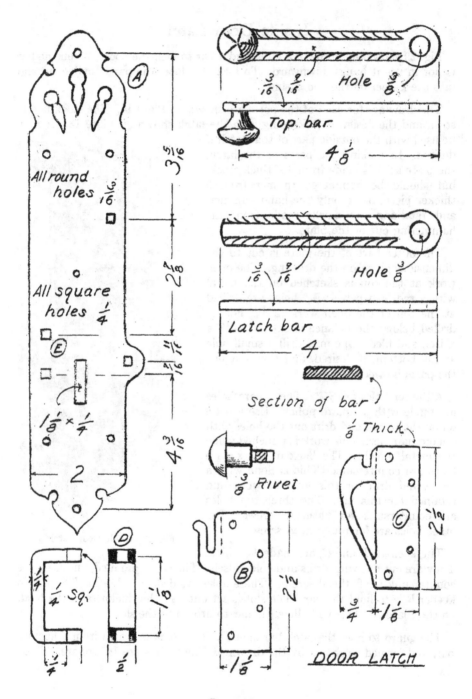

All round holes 3/16

All square holes 1/4

A

E

1 1/8 × 1/4

2

3 5/16

2 3/8

1/16 1 1/4

1/16 1 1/4

4 3/16

Hole 3/8

3/16   9/16

Top bar

4 1/8

Hole 3/8

3/16   9/16

Latch bar

4

Section of bar

1/8 Thick

3/8 Rivet

D

1/4

1/4 Sq.

1/4

1/2

1 1/8

B

2 1/2

1 1/8

C

2 1/2

3/4   1 1/8

DOOR LATCH

PLATE 14

are filed until the guard can be driven into the holes prepared for it at E. The latch bar should be tried into the guard and should not fit too tight or too loose; when fitted, it is riveted to the plate from the back.

The rivets to hold the latch bar and the top bar are made from ⅜″ round-head rivets; they are filed square at the end, so as to fit the ¼″ square holes in the plate. See drawing. File a shoulder so that, when the bars are in place and riveted, the bar will not be tight. The bars must move freely, but not too loosely. On the top of the head of the rivets, five lines are cut with a diamond-point chisel. When riveting, the heads are set onto a lead block so as not to distroy their shape.

The bars are forged from a piece large enough to make the eyes or part where the ⅜″ hole is to be drilled. A round molding is chased along the edge of the bars, a special tool being used. When using the tool, the corner of the edges of the bar is filed or ground, thus helping the tool to make the molding round. A section of the bar is shown on the drawing. To give the molding a rope effect, a small, round file is used; or a square one could be used.

The knob at the end of the top bar is forged on the round edge of the anvil. It is filed with a tenon at the end and fitted into a ⁷⁄₃₂″ hole drilled and counter-sunk in the bar. Rivet the knob into the bar; use the lead block for an anvil. Five lines are cut on the knob. One can put as much work on the knob as he cares to. It could be carved into a rosette shape, with raised parts; in fact, it and the rivets can be made very elaborate. The work is filed and smoothed with emery cloth, then lacquered.

Inside Door Lock

Fig. 30 shows a drawing for a lock to be used on a bedroom door. The lock is made in the same manner as explained for the inside part of the door latch, Fig. 29. The plate should be hammered from a thicker piece of metal to ⅛″ in thickness, to destroy the glaze on the sheet, but not to make hammer marks on the plate. If the casing around the door projects out, the bar on the plate must have a double bend so it will drop into the keeper fastened on the casing. The lock is fastened on the door with four countersunk-head screws. The keeper is screwed on the edge of the casing. One can make the plate from brass or copper with a line chased around its edge. The bar will throw over and hang down when unlocked.

Hinges

Wrought-iron hinges with a door latch and a door knocker on a door that has been made to suit them, make a very beautiful entrance to a home. Hinges are also very effective on public buildings. They give charm and beauty when worked out in keeping with the building.

Fig. 31 shows a drawing for a hinge to be worked out in soft steel. The length and size may be modified to suit the door on which it is to be placed. The drawing has been worked out for a door 1¼″ thick. The hinge consists of a butt and strap combined in one. The strap is to go on the outer part of the door, with the hinge eye on the inside, allowing the door to open in. It is to be fastened on the outside with round-head screws. The hinge butt is to have countersunk-head screws, or flatheads. The eye has three leaves. The center one is as wide as the top and bottom ones added together. The pin is to be removable and is ¼″ round.

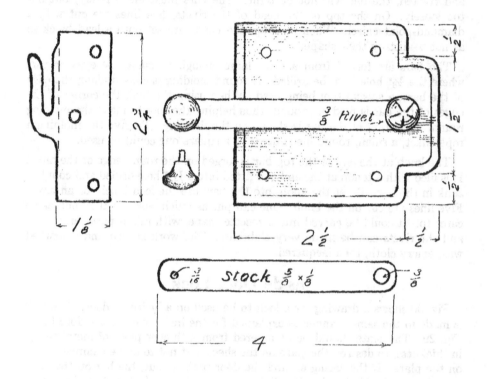

Fig. 30. Inside Door Lock

The stock is ⅛″ thick, drawn out from a heavier piece. The hinge should be made from a piece 3″ wide and as long as necessary. A loose eye is turned on one end. In doing this, a drift pin should be made from ¼″ round tool steel, about 7″ long, with both ends drawn tapering. The pin should be filed so it will measure a little less than ¼″ round in diameter.

The stock is heated on one end and bent over the edge of the anvil, curled up and around into shape. The drift is then driven through the eye, the stock being hammered tight to the pin. Make the pin straight each time it is driven in. When the pin is placed in the eye, a square should be tried along the edge of the stock to be sure that the pin and eye are at right angles, or square. If the eye is not square with the hinge, when finished, the hinge will be winding. This is important. Another important thing to remember is to have the end of the stock square before the eye is turned, also to drive the end of the stock tight on the drift pin in order to make the hole in the hinge round.

When the eye is finished, a line is scratched through the center of the strap from one end to the other. Make the line with the scratch awl or lead pencil.

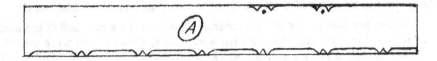

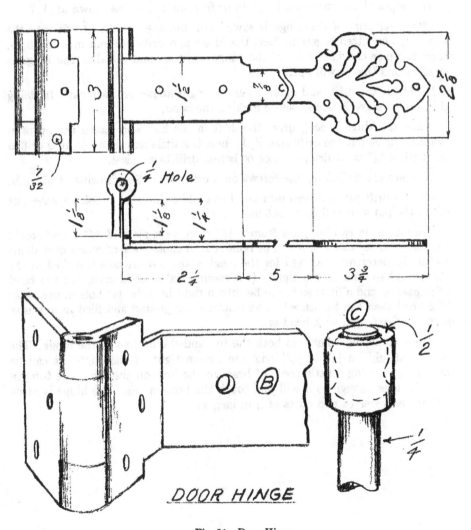

Fig. 31. Door Hinge

The shape of the strap is sketched on the metal with a red pencil. The edge and head of the strap are cut with a sharp chisel. The open work is drilled first and, when all the extra material is cut out, the open work is filed. Small saw files, ground flat on the end, make a file that will be small enough to file out the open work. The saw files are generally sharp near their ends and can be ground to any desired sizes, leaving one side that will do a lot of work.

One and one half inches in the center of the eye of the strap, half of the hinge is cut out. Saw through the eye with a hack saw, then cut the piece out with a sharp chisel, allowing enough stock so the opening can be filed to the right size.

The edges of the strap can be plain or filed on a slant, as shown at *A*.

The other part of the hinge is sawed out and the eye filed to fit into the strap. When fitted together, heat the hinge and drive the pin into the hole; then hammer the flat parts of the hinge together and see that the hinge is straight and that it will open.

Drive out the drift, and make a bend at right angles on the strap. In doing this, cool the eye in water before making the bend.

When the hinge is cool, drive the drift in the hole and fasten the butts in the vise; drive out the drift and, if the hole is a little less than $\frac{1}{4}''$, it is drilled out with a $\frac{1}{4}''$ twist drill, a brace or breast drill being used.

All holes are drilled for the screws on a drill press. See drawing of hinge *B*.

When a drift pin is driven into any holes while the stock is cold, always put oil on the pin so it will come out much easier.

The hinge pin can be made from a $\frac{1}{4}''$ rivet, or a piece of $\frac{1}{4}''$ round stock. The pin must be made so it can be removed. A short piece of round iron about $\frac{5}{16}''$ in diameter may be used for the head of the pin. A hole is drilled in the center and the pin driven tight. If a commercial rivet is used, cut the head off; upset on end a little so it can be driven tight into the $\frac{1}{4}''$ hole in the head. The head then can be brazed. The head can be ground and filed in any way seen fit. See *C*, pin with head on.

There should be a head on both the top and the bottom of the hinge. The bottom should be $\frac{1}{4}''$ or $\frac{3}{8}''$ long and driven tight. If not tight, it can be brazed by putting a little piece of brass in the hole on the pin. The top pin must be long enough so it will just touch the bottom one. The hinge is made bright and receives two coats of iron lacquer.

Lamp With Ash Tray

Fig. 32 shows a reproduction of an electric lamp with an ash tray on the lamp base. The lamp may be used as a night lamp or can be set on a table in any part of the house where a soft decorative light is wanted.

The lamp is made from soft steel with a copper shade. There are three important parts to the lamp: the base, the socket and copper ash tray, and the shade and the bracket to hold the shade. The socket is a G. E. fluted electrolier lamp-holder, push-button type, with $\frac{1}{8}''$ cap.

Fig. 32. Lamp with Ash Tray

The base, *A*, Plate 15, is made from No. 16 soft steel. The pattern for it is at *B*. The pattern may be drawn on the metal or cut from heavy paper and laid on the metal. The metal is cut with thin sharp chisels, then filed, the corners being made round. To bend the ends and sides of the base, the ends are caught in the vise and the sheet laid over and hammered to sharpen the corner. After the ends are formed, the sides are bent over in a similar way. To do this will require a piece of 1″ square iron the length of the inside of the base. The piece of iron is caught with the side of the base in the vise, and the base pulled over it. The corners do not need to be sharp; a trifle round will appear better.

The sides of the base should now measure in height $1\frac{1}{4}''$. The bottom of the sides are bent outward over the rounded edge of an anvil, the sides being made 1″ high. On one end of the top of the base, a hole is drilled and threaded with a $\frac{1}{8}''$ pipe tap. A $\frac{1}{8}''$ pipe is to be screwed into the hole to receive the lamp socket. A lock nut, C, made from $\frac{1}{8}''$ thick stock, is tightened under the base to hold the pipe.

On the other end of the base a hole is cut out to hold a copper ash tray. In cutting this hole, a series of small holes are drilled around the inside of the $3\frac{1}{2}''$ diameter, and then the inner piece cut out with a narrow chisel; the edge is smoothed with a file. The copper tray is to fit into this hole. The outer diameter of the tray is $5''$.

The tray may be hammered on wood forms or in a cast-iron die made on a machine lathe just the right size. A copper angle corner plate may be riveted over each of the corners of the sides of the base if desired. However, this is not necessary, as the base will be strong enough without the corner pieces and will appear very well without them.

The base should be tried on the surface plate to see that it is level.

The bracket to hold the shade is made from soft steel. With a piece of chalk or soapstone, the construction lines of the bracket, D, are drawn full size on the surface plate. A piece of $\frac{3}{8}''$ square iron may be upset on the end, or a $\frac{1}{2}''$ square bar may be used. The leaf end is flattened out by hammering it from one side in a $\frac{3}{16}''$ half-round anvil swage to form the center rib. The balance of the stock is drawn to size shown on the drawing. All forgings of this kind should have the sharp corners hammered off. The bracket is bent to fit the drawing on the surface plate and the hook at the end bent up.

The bracket is smoothed with a file to destroy all corners; also the center rib is filed to a point at its top end. The scallops along the edge of the leaf are made with a round file. Three holes are drilled at the bottom of the leaf. The middle one is a $\frac{5}{16}''$ hole, countersunk a little on the outside of the leaf. This hole is for the wires to go through to the lamp socket. The two $\frac{5}{32}''$ holes are for riveting the bracket to the base. In fastening these together, the bracket is held against the base and one of the $\frac{5}{32}''$ holes is marked and drilled. The $\frac{5}{16}''$ hole is then drilled through the base and countersunk on the inside to protect the lamp cord from being cut.

The $\frac{5}{32}''$ rivets may be drawn out from a larger bar. This is done by heating the bar and forging the rivets with a hammer. The pieces are cut off and, with a vise heading tool, a head is made. The rivets are put through from the inside and headed on the outside with a rivet set.

To make the copper shade, a pattern is drawn on paper or directly on the copper. It is cut out with tin snips. A piece of tapered square iron is fastened in the vise, and the copper is bent over it to form the corners. There should be $\frac{1}{4}''$ extra stock for the lap at the back of the shade to rivet the seam. Small copper rivets made from copper wire are used. These can be headed by using the vise heading tool. The riveting is done from the outside with a rivet set.

The shade is trued up by hammering it with a polished-face hammer, while it is held on a piece of pointed square iron fastened in the vise.

The shade is now hung on the hook to see that it hangs over the light bulb, which must be a small one. Use a 15-watt bulb.

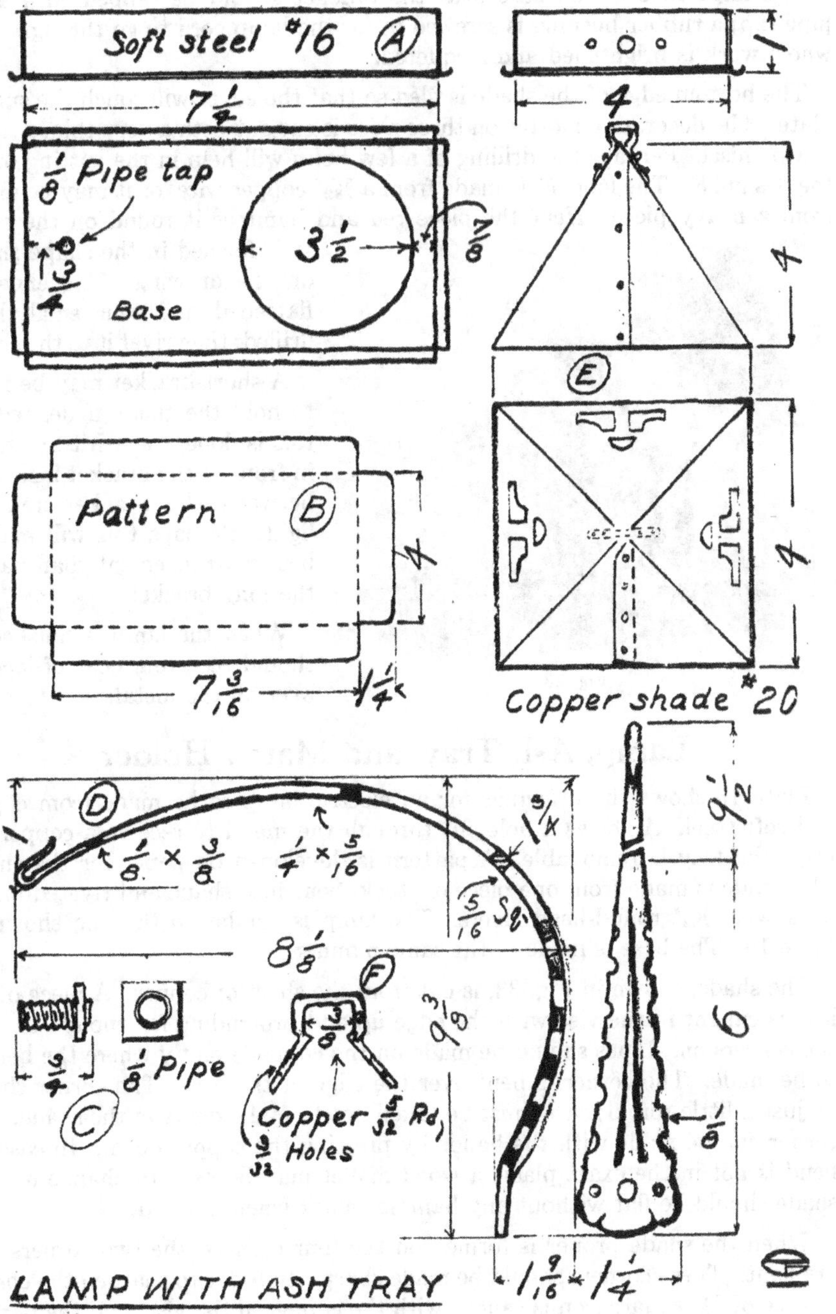
Soft steel #16
A
$7\frac{1}{4}$
4
1
$\frac{1}{8}$ Pipe tap
$\frac{3}{4}$
Base
$3\frac{1}{2}$
$\frac{7}{8}$
4
E
4
Copper shade #20
Pattern
B
4
$7\frac{3}{16}$
$1\frac{1}{4}$
D
1
$\frac{1}{8} \times \frac{3}{8}$
$\frac{1}{4} \times \frac{5}{16}$
$1\frac{3}{4}$
$\frac{5}{16}$ Sq.
$8\frac{1}{8}$
$9\frac{3}{8}$
$9\frac{1}{2}$
6
F
$\frac{3}{8}$
$\frac{3}{4}$
$\frac{1}{8}$ Pipe
C
Copper $\frac{5}{32}$ Rd.
$\frac{3}{32}$ Holes
$\frac{1}{8}$
$1\frac{9}{16}$
$1\frac{1}{4}$
LAMP WITH ASH TRAY

PLATE 15

The large hole in the base near the bracket should be tapped with a $\frac{1}{8}''$ pipe tap; a rubber bushing is screwed in for the lamp cord to go through. The whole work is brightened and lacquered.

The bottom edge of the shade is filed so that the edges will touch the surface plate. The decorative motive on three sides is cut out with a very thin, narrow, sharp chisel. Perhaps the drilling of a few holes will help in the cutting out of the design, E. The loop, F, is made from a $\frac{5}{32}''$ copper wire, or it may be drawn from a heavy piece. Heat the piece red and hammer it round on the anvil.

Fig. 33

It is formed in the shape shown on the drawing. The ends are flattened and four small holes drilled; then rivet it to the shade.

A short bracket may be made to hold the shade if desired. If this is done, the ash tray will be in front of the bracket instead of between the bracket and the light. Perhaps this will make a better arrangement than having the long bracket.

When the lamp is finished, it should receive a coat of lacquer over all the metal.

Lamp, Ash Tray, and Match Holder

Plate 16 shows the drawings for an electric lamp to be made from copper and soft steel. A shows a hole cut through the metal to receive a copper ash tray; the tray is removable. A pattern is developed on paper for the shade. The shade is made from one piece of stock, bent into shape and riveted on the back with $\frac{3}{32}''$ round-head rivets. The lamp is similar to the one shown on Plate 15. The base is made in the same manner.

The shade, shown in Fig. 33, is cut from the sheet of copper. A piece of flat iron is caught in the vise with the edge up and protruding far enough to bend the corners on. Lines should be made on the copper exactly where the bend is to be made. The corner is bent over the edge of the iron. The corner should be just a little round; care must be taken not to make dents in the shade. The corner can be made with the hands by pressing the copper down. In case the bend is not in the exact place, a wood mallet may be used to change it. The shade should be flat without any hammer mark when finished.

When the shade proper is formed on the four corners, the two corners at B are bent. These corners should be made sharp. In order to sharpen the corner, a piece of $\frac{1}{8}''$ square iron is caught with the copper in the vise, and the part, B, is hammered over on the iron to make the corner sharp. A light hammer should be used to close down the metal at B, as it will bulge outward at that

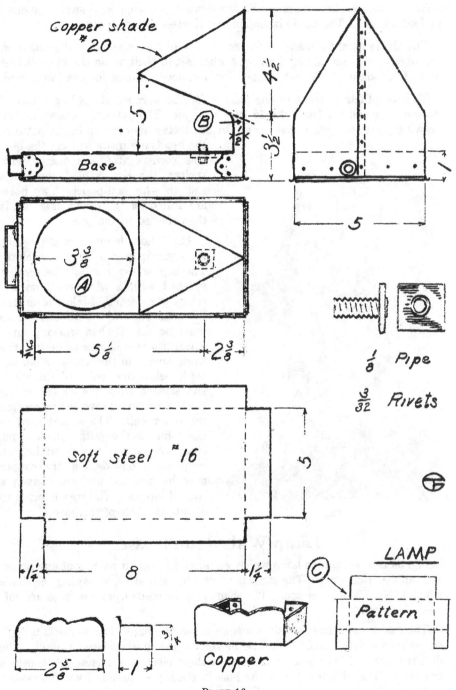

PLATE 16

point. However, there must not be any dents in the copper; if any, they must be filed smooth. The shade is lapped and riveted with $\frac{3}{32}''$ rivets.

The shade must be made to fit the outside of the base. It is then filed on the edges and made to stand straight when set in position on the base. Rivet rear of the base. It is then tapped for a rubber bushing for the lamp cord.

The receptacle in front of the base is for the purpose of holding a box of matches. It is made from No. 18 gauge copper. The pattern is shown on the drawing plate; also the dimensions. On the dotted lines shown in the pattern, the bends are made to form the box. The corners at C are brazed with spelter; the box is filed and made smooth with sandpaper. Two holes are drilled for $\frac{3}{32}''$ rivets. The box is then riveted to the base.

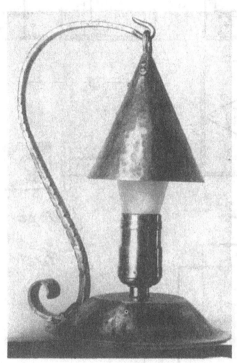

Fig. 34

The whole lamp is made bright with sandpaper and emery cloth. The copper shade should be scratch brushed with a wire wheel on the emery wheel stand. Make the scratch lines run one way—vertically. Care must be taken when working on a wheel; there is danger of getting the work caught in the wheel. Hold the work below the center of the wheel and scratch from the center of the shade downward; reverse and scratch the other half. The socket used in the lamp is the push-button type. Coat the whole lamp with iron lacquer. If one desires, the copper may be oxidized and then given a coat of lacquer. The tray is made to fit into the hole of the base.

Lamp With Round Base

Fig. 34 shows a simple lamp which would add to the furnishing of any home. It is an electrical lamp. The lamp is made from soft steel, excepting the shade which is No. 22 gauge copper. The shade may be made from No. 22 gauge soft steel if desired.

The base is made from a disk of soft steel, No. 18 gauge. The diameter is $6\frac{5}{8}''$; or perhaps a little larger would be better for the inexperienced worker. The disk is heated all over to a white heat. A short piece of 4″ steam pipe is set on the anvil. The disk is set over the hole in the pipe—directly over the center. A 12″ x 2½″ pipe is set on the disk and a piece of heavy flat iron 24″ long is

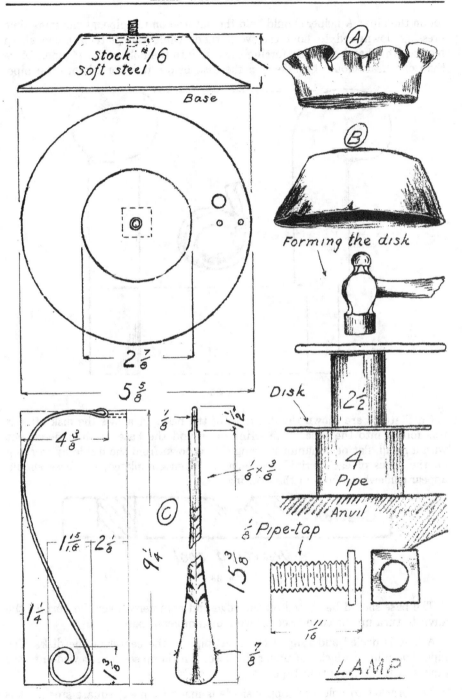

Stock #16
Soft steel

Base

$2\frac{7}{8}$

$5\frac{5}{8}$

$4\frac{3}{8}$

$1\frac{15}{16}$ $2\frac{1}{8}$ $9\frac{1}{4}$

$1\frac{1}{4}$

$\frac{3}{8}$

$\frac{1}{8}$ $\frac{1}{2}$

$\frac{1}{8} \times \frac{3}{8}$

$15\frac{3}{8}$

$\frac{7}{8}$

(A)

(B)

Forming the disk

Disk

$2\frac{1}{2}$

4
Pipe

Anvil

$\frac{1}{8}$ Pipe-tap

$\frac{11}{16}$

LAMP

PLATE 17

set on the pipe. A helper should hold the flat iron on the pipe, at the same time pressing downward to hold the work rigid; while the plate is given sharp blows with a hand hammer, forcing the disk into the hole in the 4″ pipe. More than one heat should be taken on the disk before it is forced into the pipe.

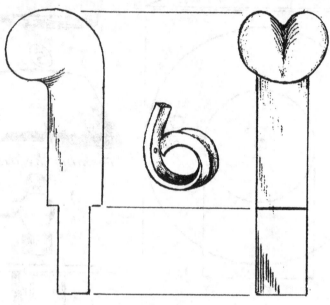

Fig. 35

On Plate 17 are shown the drawings of the base. A shows the disk after it was forced into the pipe. The wrinkles around the base are hammered out with a small, flat peen hammer, being closed down from the inside by working on the edges of each wrinkle while hot. When completed, the base should appear somewhat like B in the drawing.

Fig. 36

The base should be heated on the edge and hammered over the horn of the anvil to turn up the edge. See drawing of completed base.

A hole is drilled and tapped for a ⅛″ pipe in the center of the disk. The pipe should have a lock nut under the base. The lamp socket screwed onto the pipe is of the push-button type.

The bracket to hold the copper shade is made from ⅜″ square stock. It is hammered flat on one end. The balance of the bar is forged ⅛″ x ⅜″ and the top end is drawn ⅛″ round for the hook. The chasing on the bracket, *C*, is made with a diamond-point chisel or file. The lines are short diagonals on both sides. The entire length and shape of the bracket is shown on the drawing plate.

The leaf end is formed by hammering it on a special tool, Fig. 35. The tool is made to fasten in the vise. Heat the end of the bracket and, with a flat peen hammer, drive the metal into the depression of the tool, at the same time bending it into volute form.

A drawing of the bracket is made full size with a piece of soapstone or chalk, the dimensions shown on the plate being used.

When the bracket is shaped, two holes are drilled. The best way to locate them is to hold the bracket against the base, mark and drill ⁵⁄₃₂″ holes; then set the bracket against the base again and mark the holes to be drilled into the base. The rivet heads are made by using the vise heading tool. When riveting the bracket to the base, the heads are on the outside and are riveted on the inside of the base. A 6″ long, ⅜″ square piece of iron, with a depression in the center, is used to hold the heads of the rivets while riveting the two pieces together, Fig. 36. The piece is put through the scroll and on the top of the open vise with the head of the rivet in the depression while hammering the rivet on the inside of the base.

The hook at the top of the bracket should be directly over the lamp socket so that the shade will cover the socket. The lamp should be set on the surface plate to make the bracket stand straight: use the square to try the work.

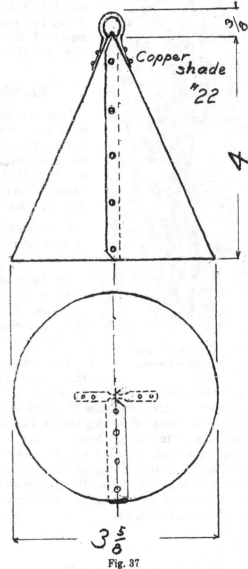

Copper shade #22

Fig. 37

The pattern of the shade is developed on the metal and cut out with a pair of snips. The drawing is shown in Fig. 37. The stock is then bent over the horn of the anvil, also over a smaller piece of round iron, until the laps are just right. Holes are drilled for small rivets, which can be made from copper or iron wire by using the vise heading tool. When the shade is riveted, it is then trued up and made round.

Fig. 38. Outside Door Knocker

The loop at the top is made from ⅛" or ⁵⁄₃₂" round stock and flattened on each end with holes drilled and piece riveted on. The whole lamp is smoothed with emery cloth until bright. It is then given a coat of iron lacquer.

Outside Door Knockers

Door knockers are used to rap on the door in order to attract the attention of those who live inside. They are used mostly on homes. They are used instead of a door bell, and are much more practical because they do not get out of order. When made well and fastened to a suitable door, they are very attractive.

Door knockers are made from brass, cast iron, or wrought iron, and in early times were extensively used.

Fig. 38 shows a reproduction of a simple door knocker. Plate 18 shows the drawings with dimensions. The knocker is to be made from soft steel. It consists of two principal parts: the plate to be screwed to the door, and the hammer.

The hammer should be made first, for the reason that, if it should be a little long or short, the plate could be made to suit it. A piece of ¾" square stock is used to make the hammer. A shows drawings of the different rough forgings of the grotesque head. Four steps in making the head are illustrated. The first one shows the bar forged into a rough form; the next one shows the leaf form split back toward the head. This is done with a long, thin hand hot chisel made from an old file. In splitting the piece, it is heated, caught in a vise, then split from the back towards the head. It is important to end the split exactly in the right place. A chisel mark along the outside would help; it would act as a guide for the hot chisel to follow.

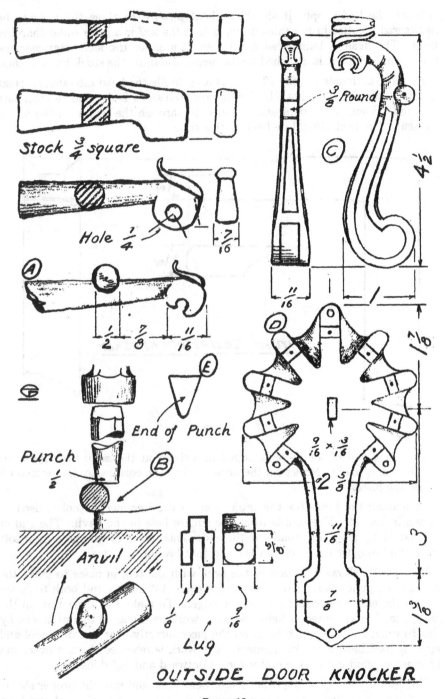

Stock ¾ square

Hole ¼

⅞ Round

ⒸC

4½

7/16

Ⓐ

½   ⅞   11/16

Ⓖ

Ⓔ

End of Punch

Punch ½

ⒷB

Anvil

⅝

Lug

⅛   9/16

Ⓓ

1⅞

9/16 × 3/16

2⅝

11/16

3

⅞

3⅜

1

7/16

OUTSIDE DOOR KNOCKER

PLATE 18

When the leaf is split it should be bent upward to allow the neck to be hammered. Notice in the third drawing that the leaf is a little wider than the head. The head is hammered a little smaller under the leaf. Hammer the neck round where it is attached to the head; also draw the stock back farther.

A half-oval double-cut file 12″ long is used to file the head into shape. Heat the work and file while hot. Under the leaf, the stock is flat and the top part is round. When cool a depression is chiseled through the center on the top of the leaf. The neck should be bent at this time.

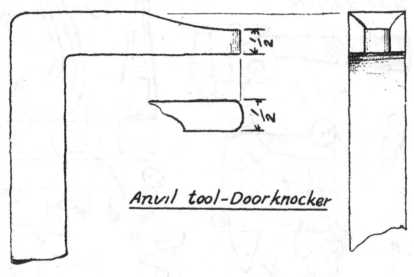

Anvil tool-Doorknocker

Fig. 39

The other end of the piece is forged into shape at the same time the bend in the neck is made. Notice on the drawing that the corners are hammered off below the hinge.

In making the hinge, or the projection on the hammer, a tool is used as shown in Fig. 39. The tool is to fit the square hole in the anvil. The end of the tool is ½″ x ½″ and round at the end. This tool may be made from soft steel—and roughly made, except the end that lays on the anvil.

B, Plate 18, shows a section of the neck with the tool in place to make the hinge. The punch is the same size as the tool—½″ exact—and both tools are flat on the end surface and have sharp edges. To make the projection on the neck, the piece is heated, a helper sets the work on the anvil tool as shown by the drawing, and the punch is set on the piece directly over the anvil tool and given a good blow with the hammer. The work is reheated, turned over, and hammered again until the metal is forced outward and ⅛″ thick.

The leaf at the top of the head is now bent back and into the proper shape. A ¼″ hole is drilled for the mouth. The drawing on the plate shows lines which mark where to saw out the metal, or the place may be filed to make the mouth open. When the hammer is cool, it is dressed by filing and, if the hinge part needs straightening, it is done with a chisel and file.

Lines are now chased on the knocker with a small cold chisel. The neck lines are made with a file. When marking the lines on the knocker, use a gauge. The lines around the mouth are best made with the diamond point.

The back plate, D, is made from 1/8" stock. The shape is drawn on the metal with a red pencil and then cut out. The edges are ground and filed. The metal is sunk down at the top of the plate, as shown by the shading on the drawing. This is done with a hand punch while the metal is hot. E shows the shape of the end of a punch. The end of a punch should be a trifle smaller than the finished work, as the metal will stretch. When this operation is completed, the edges are again filed to reshape them. The center hole is drilled and cut square with a chisel or file. The back of the hole is countersunk.

Lines are chased on the plate, and screw holes are drilled for round-head wood screws.

The lug is made by forging a piece of stock 7/16" x 1/16" square. A slot is cut with a file 1/8" wide so that the projection on the hammer will fit into it, forming a hinge and letting the hammer move back and forth. The tenon is also filed to fit the hole in the plate. Sometimes the lug is brazed with brass, to make it more firm. However, if brazed, one should be careful to use very little brass, because it stains the metal. The brass should be put on the back side. In doing this, care must be taken or the lug may become too hot.

Fig. 40. Iron Knocker

The plate is now ready to receive the hammer. It should be fitted into place and a 5/32" hole drilled through both pieces; the hole must be straight. A 5/32" pin is put through the hole and two half-oval washers on the pin. These washers should be made large enough to cover the lug and hide the joint. They are countersunk and the pin is riveted from each side. Do not countersink the washers very much, because it will be hard to fill the space when riveting. A file should be used to smooth the rivet ends. The washers may be decorated by cutting lines with the diamond point.

If the hammer should be very tight when riveted, heat the neck to a dark red and work the hammer until it is free.

The knocker is smoothed with a file and emery cloth until bright; then lacquer two coats all over the work. All the work shown in this book should be completely lacquered, not just a part of it.

Fig. 41. Wrought-iron Knocker

The hammer of the outside door knocker shown at Fig. 40 has been forged from one piece of soft steel; there is no welding. The head is made by heating a piece of stock and splitting the mouth on each side of the tongue. The leaf forms on the top and the bottom of the head are also split. The design is then worked out with the hammer. The top jaw and the under one are bent away from the tongue; the tongue is then drawn out. At the bottom of the hammer, a collar is welded when the knocker is worked out and it begins to take form. A large double-cut file is used to file the work while hot. When cool, the head is chiseled and chased with various kinds of tools.

Fig. 41 shows an outside door knocker. It is made from soft steel. The plate is ⅛″ thick. The nails are made by welding heads on wood screws, then dressing the heads with a file and chiseling to decorate them. A large, separate piece is riveted in the center of the plate to reinforce the lug which holds the ring.

The ring is forged from one piece of stock; the leaf form is split while hot. The upper half of the ring was forged square, then heated and twisted. A half-oval double-cut file is used to rough the work while it is hot. After it is cool, it is filed and chiseled with various kinds of chisels.

Inside Door Knocker

Plate 19 shows a drawing for a knocker that may be used on a bedroom door. This kind of knocker should be quite small, with the hammer close to the plate and with nothing protruding that might catch anything.

At *A* is the drawing with dimensions. The stock is soft steel; the plate is ⅛″ thick; a thicker piece may be used. If so, it should be heated and hammered until it is about ⅛″ or less. If ⅛″ is used, hammer it a little thinner.

A paper pattern of the design for the back plate is made; or, if one can draw quite well, the design is sketched directly on the metal. Notice that the plate is made much larger at the top than at the bottom. This is done in order to give the design variety—larger top and small bottom. The plate is cut cold with a hand chisel on the outside of the line; the loops under the top are drilled.

The open work is drilled and cut out with a narrow chisel, then filed. The bottom of the plate has a line chased near the edge. The gauge is used to mark the line. A small, narrow chisel is used to cut the line. The metal around the volutes are sunk down as shown by the shading on the drawing. This is done with a short flat-end punch. It may be sunk while the plate is cold, or it may be heated to a dark red, then a longer tool used to set the metal down thinner on the edge. This brings the volute into relief. All of the holes are ⁷⁄₃₂″. The center hole for the lug is drifted out square to ¼″. Always use oil on the punch when drifting cold metal. The hole in the plate to receive the lug is countersunk on the back side. This is done with the brace and countersink.

In making the lug, ½″ square stock is used. The slot to receive the hammer is filed ¼″, or perhaps a little more. The square tenon is filed ¼″ square and

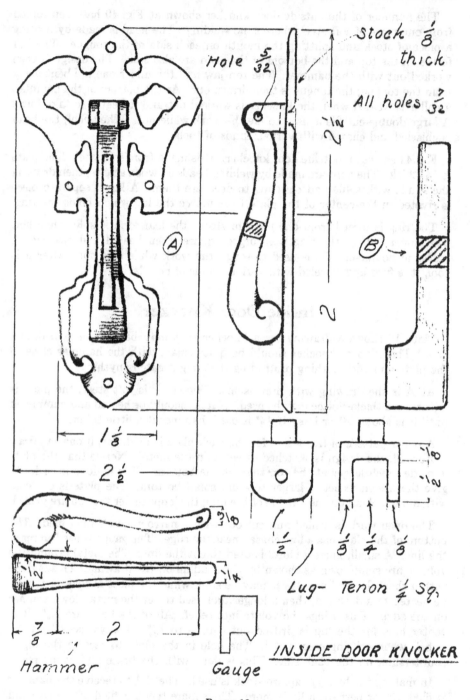

Hole $\frac{5}{32}$

stock $\frac{1}{8}$ thick

All holes $\frac{7}{32}$

$2\frac{1}{2}$

2

Ⓐ

Ⓑ

$1\frac{1}{8}$

$2\frac{1}{2}$

$\frac{3}{8}$

$\frac{1}{2}$

$\frac{1}{4}$

$\frac{7}{8}$

2

Hammer

Gauge

$\frac{1}{2}$

$\frac{1}{8}$

$\frac{1}{2}$

$\frac{3}{8}$ $\frac{1}{4}$ $\frac{3}{8}$

Lug- Tenon $\frac{1}{4}$ Sq.

INSIDE DOOR KNOCKER

PLATE 19

$\frac{5}{16}''$ long. The lug is put into the hole in the plate and riveted. If, when the lug is fitted into the hole, and before riveting, it is heated and laid on the forge to cool and anneal, it will be softer and therefore easier to rivet.

The hammer is forged from $\frac{5}{8}''$ square stock. The large end or ball is made by heating the end of the stock, then letting it protrude past the outer edge of the anvil and hammering it so it will appear as at B. The end is now rounded and bent as shown by the drawing. The balance of the hammer is drawn to the right size and length.

Notice the corner at the top end; it is rounded a little. This can be done with a file. It is made round so that, when in place, it will turn readily in the lug. A line is chased on the front of the hammer, also on the side of the ball. When doing this use a small chisel, the piece having been fastened in the vise between two pieces of copper. File the corners so there are no sharp edges. In chasing the lines on the front of the hammer, a gauge is used to mark the lines before they are cut.

The hammer is fitted into the lug and a $\frac{5}{32}''$ hole drilled through. Care must be taken to drill the hole straight. Perhaps the work should be clamped onto an angle plate before drilling. The lug is countersunk with the brace and countersink bit. To make the pin, a piece of stock is forged about $\frac{5}{32}''$ round, filed, and driven into the hole. The pin is cut the proper length on each end, filed flat, and riveted.

If the hammer is too tight, heat the lug and work the hammer until it is free.

The whole knocker is relieved of all sharp edges and corners with a smooth file and emery cloth. The knocker must be smooth so that there is no danger of injuring the hands. When finished, it is lacquered. It is to be fastened on the door with round-head screws; these should be brightened on the heads and lacquered.

Smoking Stand and Tobacco Box

A smoking stand with tobacco box is shown at Fig. 42. A movable ash tray is shown on the second shelf. The tray is to hold ash from the pipe. The box holds the tobacco. The top and bottom shelves of the stand are turned up on the edge to form large trays. The stand is to be placed near a chair when in use. The stand is made simple. There are no sharp places or corners to interfere with use, and it can be cleaned easily.

The stand consists of four legs, the top tray, and the lower one. It is made from soft steel. The movable tray on the second shelf may be made from No. 20 copper. The tobacco box is soft steel with copper legs and copper handle on the cover. The rivets are copper through the iron, and iron through the copper.

Plate 20 shows the drawings for the stand. The legs are made from $\frac{1}{2}''$ square stock. They are heated and hammered from one side and allowed to become about $\frac{5}{8}''$ wide and $\frac{11}{32}''$ thick. They should be alike and forged with

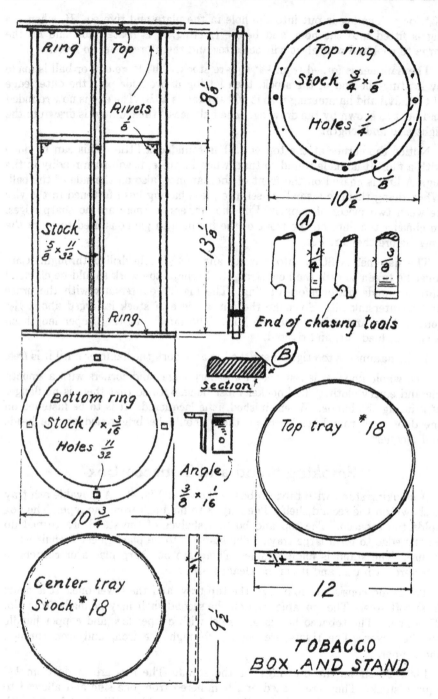

Ring   Top

Rivets
$\frac{1}{8}$

Stock
$\frac{5}{8} \times \frac{11}{32}$

Ring

$8\frac{5}{8}$

$13\frac{5}{8}$

Top ring

Stock $\frac{3}{4} \times \frac{1}{8}$

Holes $\frac{1}{4}$

$\frac{1}{8}$

$10\frac{1}{2}$

(A)

$\frac{1}{4}$

$\frac{3}{8}$

End of chasing tools

(B)

Section

Bottom ring

Stock $1 \times \frac{3}{16}$

Holes $\frac{11}{32}$

$10\frac{3}{4}$

Angle
$\frac{3}{8} \times \frac{1}{16}$

Top tray   *18

12

Center tray
Stock *18

$9\frac{1}{2}$

TOBACCO
BOX AND STAND

PLATE 20

the hand hammer. The legs have a round molding chased on each edge. The molding is made with chasing tools. The cutting edge of the narrow one is $\frac{1}{4}''$ wide; the other one is $\frac{3}{8}''$. See A. The corners on the two edges of the bar are ground. See B. This is done to assist the tool to make the molding round. To make the molding, the $\frac{1}{4}''$ wide chasing tool is used while the metal is cold. The gauge on the tool is set against the edge of the bar. While in this position strike the tool with the hand hammer as it is moved along the bar.

When the molding is well formed, the bar is heated to a dark red and, using quick, light blows of the hammer, the $\frac{3}{8}''$ wide tool is chased along the edge until the molding is round. The tenon on each end of the bars is filed; the top one is $\frac{1}{4}''$ round, and the bottom one is $1\frac{1}{32}''$ square. The little angles to hold the lower shelf are made from $\frac{1}{16}''$ x $\frac{3}{8}''$ stock. These should be riveted to the legs with $\frac{1}{8}''$ round-head rivets.

The stock for the top ring is drawn out to $\frac{3}{4}''$ x $\frac{1}{8}''$. Heat the bar, and bend on the edge over the horn of the anvil to the correct size; then weld. It is best to weld the ring a little small and stretch to the correct dimensions. Make the bottom one from stock $1''$ x $\frac{3}{16}.''$

The holes are located on the top ring and drilled with $\frac{1}{8}''$ and $\frac{1}{4}''$ drills. Clamp the two rings together and drill through the $\frac{1}{4}''$ holes into the bottom ring. Before the clamps are released, center punch a mark on each ring so, when they are assembled, the holes will be in the right position with the top side up.

The holes in the bottom ring are drilled out $\frac{5}{16}''$. The holes are countersunk on the

Fig. 42. Smoking Stand and Tobacco Box

bottom side and made square to fit the tenon on the bottom of the legs. The holes in the top ring are countersunk on the top side of the ring so that, when the legs are riveted, the ring will be flat on the top.

The legs are riveted into the bottom ring first and must be made to stand vertical. This is very important, in order that the top ring will fit onto the legs without straining them. The best way to know when the legs are vertical

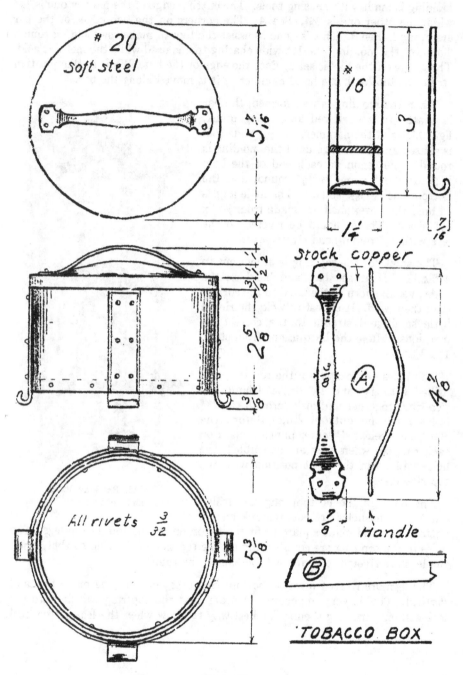

#20
Soft steel

#16

Stock copper

$\textcircled{A}$

Handle

$\textcircled{B}$

All rivets $\frac{3}{32}$

TOBACCO BOX

PLATE 21

is to set the work on the surface plate and try them with a two-foot square. The top ring has eight ⅛″ holes drilled in it to rivet the top to. The ring should be set onto the legs and riveted tight.

The top and lower trays are made from No. 18 soft steel. The disk for the top one is 12⅝″ in diameter; the lower one is 10⅛″. The disks are cut out with a sharp cold chisel. Describe a circle on the metal and cut on the line. An inner circle should also be made and then bend the edge over on this line as shown on the drawing.

In bending the edge over at right angles, the work is hammered while cold. A curved bar of iron is fastened vertically in the vise, and the stock is hammered over the edge of the bar. One must bend very little at one time with a small hammer. A little practice is all one needs to hammer the edge over. Where the edge is bent it is filed smooth. The height may be ¼″ or more.

Fig. 43. Tobacco Box

The top is set on the stand in the right position and, with a slim scratch awl, the locations of the holes are marked through the holes in the ring. The trays are riveted in place, ⅛″ rivets being used—eight rivets through the ring and four through the angles for the lower tray. The stand when finished should be smoothed with a file and emery cloth.

The top and inner shelves can be made from No. 16 copper, if desired. The top is cut out the proper size, then hammered with a polished hammer. The hammering is best done on a smooth surface plate—one that has been polished. The copper is made flat by hammering with a wood mallet. The rim is made by bending the edges at right angles over the end of a polished iron bar fastened in a vise. The shelves are riveted in place with ⅛″ copper rivets. The rivets should be with countersink heads so that the shelves and rivet heads are smooth.

Fig. 43 shows the tobacco box, and Plate 21 gives the drawing of the box with dimensions. The box is made from No. 20 soft steel. The stock for the cylinder is cut 16½″ x 3″. The cylinder is formed by bending the piece over a steam pipe until the edges are butted together. They are held in place with binding wire until brazed.

In brazing the cylinder with spelter or brass wire, it is heated to a dark red. Fine borax is put on the inside and also on the outside of the joint. The spelter is put on the inside and the joint reheated until the spelter flows. It is best to braze one half of the joint, then reverse and braze the other half.

When cool, the work is made round on the pipe or a wooden mandrel. To do this, on a piece of paper describe a circle the diameter of the outside of the cylinder. When making the work round, try it on the circle to be sure it becomes round. If the cylinder is not round on the top, the cover will not remove freely. File the joint smooth inside and also on the outside.

The bottom is made from No. 20 soft steel. A disk is cut about 6″ in diameter and ground on the edge. An inner circle is described with the diameter the size of the inside of the box. With a short bar of iron, flat on the end, and fastened vertically in the vise, bend the edge at right angles in the same manner as described in the making of the top for the stand. Bend about ¼″ of the edge. The bottom is pressed into the cylinder and riveted, copper rivets being used.

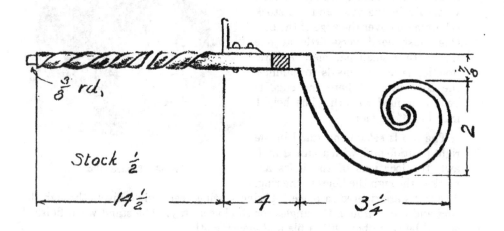

Fig. 44

The cover is made from No. 20 soft steel. The disk should be cut about 7″ in diameter. The cover is bumped up about ⅜″ in the center. An inner circle is described with a diameter the size of the outside of the box; also another circle with diameter ⅜″ greater than the inner one. The edge is then ground to the outer line.

The stock on the outside of the inner line is bent at right angles. The best way to do this is to hammer the edge cold around the cover on the line. It is then heated and a small part hammered at one time with the face of a small cross-peen riveting hammer. The wrinkles are hammered out on an anvil with the peen of the hammer. When the cover is finished, the copper handle is made.

The handle is cut out with thin, sharp chisels. A heavy piece of copper will make a better-looking handle. One can be forged, the center of the handle being left heavier, and the outer part thinner where it is fastened to the cover. The drawing, A, for the handle is fastened with small iron rivets. One can purchase ³⁄₃₂″ round rivets or make them. The legs are made from No. 16 copper. A line may be chased around the edges. For this, a special tool, B, is used. The gauge on the tool is made very short. It is important to have the edges of the legs filed straight before the line is made. The legs are fastened with iron rivets, each side of the joint. Brighten with emery cloth and lacquer.

Fig. 44 shows a drawing for a leg that may be used for a smoking stand similar to the one at Plate 20. The inner tray for this leg is placed below the center of the stand, instead of above. It is to have one ring at the top. The bottom tray, instead of a ring at the bottom, binds the stand. The bottom of the leg is bent into a scroll. The little angle to hold the lower tray has four holes for $\frac{1}{8}''$ rivets. The stock for legs is $\frac{1}{2}''$ square soft steel, twisted to relieve the plain surface of the legs. The stand is constructed in the same manner as explained in Plate 20.

Fig. 45 shows a finished stand. The legs are made from soft steel 1″ x $\frac{1}{4}''$. The ring at the top is made from $1\frac{1}{8}''$ x $\frac{3}{16}''$ soft steel. Four square-cornered holes, $\frac{3}{4}''$ x $\frac{1}{4}''$, are made in the ring. The legs are riveted into the ring. The top tray and the lower one are made from No. 18 gauge copper. The top tray is riveted onto the ring with copper rivets; the lower one is riveted to small, soft steel angles fastened to the legs.

Fig. 45